BONHOEFFER:
A GUIDE FOR THE PERPLEXED

T&T Clark *Guides for the Perplexed*

T&T Clark's Guides for the Perplexed are clear, concise and accessible introductions to thinkers, writers and subjects that students and readers can find especially challenging. Concentrating specifically on what it is that makes the subject difficult to grasp, these books explain and explore key themes and ideas, guiding the reader towards a thorough understanding of demanding material.

***Guides for the Perplexed* available from T&T Clark:**

De Lubac: A Guide for the Perplexed, David Grumett
Christian Bioethics: A Guide for the Perplexed, Agneta Sutton
Calvin: A Guide for the Perplexed, Paul Helm
Tillich: A Guide for the Perplexed, Andrew O'Neill
The Trinity: A Guide for the Perplexed, Paul M. Collins
Christology: A Guide for the Perplexed, Alan Spence
Wesley: A Guide for the Perplexed, Jason E. Vickers
Pannenberg: A Guide for the Perplexed, Timothy Bradshaw
Balthasar: A Guide for the Perplexed, Rodney Howsare
Theological Anthropology: A Guide for the Perplexed, Marc Cortez

Forthcoming titles:

Benedict XVI: A Guide for the Perplexed, Tracey Rowland
Interfaith Relations: A Guide for the Perplexed, Jeffrey Bailey
Eucharist: A Guide for the Perplexed, Ralph N. McMichael

BONHOEFFER: A GUIDE FOR THE PERPLEXED

JOEL LAWRENCE

t&t clark

Published by T&T Clark International

A Continuum Imprint
The Tower Building, 11 York Road, London SE1 7NX
80 Maiden Lane, Suite 704, New York, NY 10038

www.continuumbooks.com

British Library Cataloguing-in-Publication Data
A catalogue record for this book is available from the British Library

ISBN: 978-0-567-03237-9 (Hardback)
978-0-567-03238-6 (Paperback)

Typeset by Newgen Imaging Systems Pvt Ltd, Chennai, India
Printed and bound in Great Britain by the MPG Books Group

CONTENTS

ACKNOWLEDGMENTS

This book has arisen out of my interactions with many people over many years who have helped me to understand more deeply that theological reflection is done in communities of dialogue, questioning, critique and, ultimately, prayer. While I cannot possibly mention each person who has encouraged me along my path, I do want to give thanks to those who had a direct hand in this book.

First, I would like to thank my colleagues on the faculty of Bethel Seminary. I am grateful for the spirit of camaraderie and openness that mark our community, and am appreciative of the formative influence that these people have had on my own life. I would like especially to acknowledge my debt to Dr. Leland Eliason, our now-retired Provost, for his continual encouragement, care, and support. I am thankful to Bethel for the sabbatical leave during the spring term of 2009 in order to finish up this project, and I appreciate the opportunity for extended time of study and reflection afforded by that break.

A part of that sabbatical leave was spent in Cambridge, England, researching and writing at Tyndale House. I am grateful to the Warden, Dr. Peter Williams, for welcoming me back to Tyndale House and providing a desk for study. Also, I am ever appreciative of the work of the Tyndale Staff, most especially Dr. Elizabeth Magba, Dr. David Instone-Brewer, and Mrs. Fiona Craig, who are so accommodating to all who come there, even systematic theologians.

My friends in the International Bonhoeffer Society have encouraged my research into Bonhoeffer's theology in innumerable ways. I am grateful for this community of pastors and scholars, and for our work of understanding, critiquing, and growing together through our common interest in Bonhoeffer. I would most especially like to thank my Twin Cities colleagues, Reverend John Matthews and Dr. Lori Brandt-Hale, for our friendship, mutual encouragement, and conversations at various restaurants around the area. In addition, I am continually grateful to Rev. Dr. Stephen Plant for his expert guidance in my research and for his continuing impact on my life. Thanks, Stephen, for the opportunity to write this book!

I owe a special debt to my research fellow, Mr. Justin Winzenburg. Thanks for all your help researching, reading, editing, and critiquing. I look forward to your future contributions to scholarship and the church.

Finally, to my family: Thank you, Myndi, for our partnership in life. There's very little that can be said here to describe the privilege I feel of being your husband.

With four young children in the house, writing can be a challenge. But 'interruptions' from Bethany, Anna, Katherine, and Micah are a joy. I am grateful for your trips into my study, as you search for gum, candy, or a hug. As you grow older, I pray that you will continue to come into my study, and I promise to keep a well-stocked supply of all of the above items. I dedicate this book to you.

CHAPTER 1

BONHOEFFER: INTRODUCING HIS LIFE AND THINKING

The academic life does not often translate into good theater. One can think of the life of Immanuel Kant, who did all of his philosophical work within the confines of Königsburg, Prussia, rarely leaving the city limits in his whole life. His life is hardly a gripping, edge-of-your-seat drama. Or, there is Rene Descartes, who accomplished his undertaking of the method of doubt while sitting in his room staring at the fire and pieces of wax. Hollywood is not exactly lining up for the rights to this story.

Of course, there are exceptions to the rule: Martin Luther's life story has elements of significant dramatic tension, and has been turned into a major motion picture, but even then, the concentration is on a short span of Luther's story, the heated years of Luther's confrontation with Rome and the ensuing firestorm he aroused; his later days, after the flames of his revolution died down and he led a more or less stable, pastoral existence, does not receive treatment in the film. Another film has immortalized the story of Thomas More, a man whose conviction and humility stand out against the antagonist of his story, Henry VIII. In each of these cases, what makes the stories interesting is not their academic study, but the way that the ideas and convictions that were born of academic study forced them into confrontations with political and social structures, as well as the personal stories of courage and fortitude that propel them into their confrontation with the forces and leaders of their day. The political circumstances of their times certainly drive their life stories, but it is their theology that drives their reactions to the political circumstances. Kant dwelt in a stable city, and his life and philosophy are a reflection of that stability. Luther dwelt in uncertain and ever-evolving times, and his story both contributes to and is a reflection of that instability. So, while the drama of their lives cannot be captured by a person's academic achievements, the result of their philosophical or theological convictions become the impetus for these persons' confrontation of and interaction with the political and cultural world in which she finds herself. This is certainly true of the subject of our study, Dietrich Bonhoeffer.

Bonhoeffer lived in tumultuous times. His life story makes good theater, and his theology is a result of and also a contributor to the shape of history in Germany in the early part of the 20th century. Bonhoeffer's theology can be easily misunderstood if not set against the backdrop of the times in which he lived. Apart from the course of his life, we cannot understand this theologian.

BIOGRAPHY

Bonhoeffer was born is Breslau, Germany, modern day Poland, on 4 February 1906. He was not alone in his arrival, being accompanied by a twin sister, Sabine.[1] Bonhoeffer's father, Karl, was an eminent psychiatrist who taught at the University of Berlin from 1912 until his retirement.[2] His mother, Paula Bonhoeffer, was descended from lawyers and theologians,[3] and reflected the learning and adroitness of mind in her lineage, often inquiring into what her theologian-son was reading and herself taking up the theological texts he was studying.[4]

Bonhoeffer and his twin sister were the sixth and seventh of eight children, their younger sister Susanne to arrive in 1909. They were preceded by three older brothers: Karl Friedrich, who became a well-known physicist, having studied under Einstein and Planck; Walter, who was killed in World War I; and Klaus. Also before them came two older sisters, Ursala and Kristel. As can be imagined, the Bonhoeffer house was a hub of activity, not only because of the number of children and people employed by the family to help with the household, but also because of Karl Bonhoeffer's profession, which brought him into contact with many of the academic leaders of the day, including theologians who would teach Bonhoeffer as a university student at Berlin. These Berlin academics spent much time in the Bonhoeffer household, holding intense conversations with Dietrich's father, a setting that undoubtedly did much to shape the mind and interests of the young Dietrich.

The decision to become a theologian came to Bonhoeffer as a teenager, and it was against the grain of his family. Although descended from theologians on his mothers' side, neither theology nor church life played a large role in his immediate familial context. It was thought that Dietrich might become a musician due to his exceptional giftsin that field, but he decided instead to become a theologian. About this decision, Bonhoeffer's friend and biographer Eberhard Bethge writes,

> At home, he made no bones about it. Even when his brothers and sisters refused to take him seriously, he did not let it disconcert him. When he was fourteen . . . they tried to convince him that . . . the church to which he proposed to devote himself was a poor, feeble, boring, petty and bourgeois institution, but he confidently replied: 'In that case I shall reform it!'[5]

Bethge suggests that Bonhoeffer's choice of occupation may have arisen out of something of a search for significance in his life:

> At the root of his choice was a basic drive toward independence. . . . The presence of theologians among his forebears made his choice of a career not that unusual; while this no doubt played a part, it was hardly a decisive factor. His isolation among his brothers and sisters was probably of far greater importance; it may have nourished his need to surpass them all.[6]

Later, Bonhoeffer himself describes his early motivation toward theology as driven by ego, reflecting on a change in his attitude toward theology in the early 1930s.[7]

Bonhoeffer's decision to study theology took him first to Tübingen in 1923–1924, and then to Berlin. In Berlin he studied with Adolph von Harnack, Karl Holl, and Reinhold Seeburg, three of the most important theologians of their day. During this time, Bonhoeffer stood out as an exceptional thinker, applying himself both to philosophy and theology. It was here, through Seeburg and Holl, that he delved deeply into Luther, who would be a considerable influence on his theology. It was also during this time that he began to read another key influence, the new Swiss theologian, Karl Barth. In many respects these two theologians, Luther and Barth, are the giants who hover in Bonhoeffer's background; we will see their role in his theology throughout this book.

Bonhoeffer completed his studies in Berlin by writing his doctoral dissertation, *Sanctorum Communio.*[8] In this text, Bonhoeffer explicates the nature of church community, engaging with social theory of the day, but focusing most clearly on the importance of a theology of revelation for coming to understand the nature of the church. After completing his thesis, Bonhoeffer pursued his ordination, taking on a curacy in Barcelona. Upon completion of this training, he returned to Berlin to compose his *Habilitationschrift, Act and Being*, a book in which Bonhoeffer engages with the question of ontology and event, seeking to find a way in which to see the church as the community in which the act of God's revelation and ontology find their unity.

Act and Being qualified Bonhoeffer to be a university lecturer, but before he would take up his teaching duties, he spent a year in the United States, as a visiting scholar at Union Theological Seminary in New York. During this time, Bonhoeffer was introduced to a variety of influences that would continue to shape his theological trajectory. The two most important are Jean Lassere, a French pacifist theologian who influenced Bonhoeffer toward a reading of the Sermon on the Mount that would take the teachings of Christ seriously, thus sparking an interest in the interpretation of the sermon that yields a pacifist conception of Christianity, and Franklin Fisher, an African-American student who invited Bonhoeffer to worship with him at Harlem's Abyssinian Baptist Church. Here, Bonhoeffer was introduced to the issues of poverty and racism in America, and recognized the significant theological issue at stake concerning the 'negro question'[9] in America. Both of these encounters would contribute to Bonhoeffer's thinking as he returned to Germany and the storm brewing in his homeland.

Upon his return to Germany, Bonhoeffer took up his teaching duties at Berlin. The lectures he conducted during his brief teaching career were varied, but demonstrate the range of topics that were interesting Bonhoeffer during his continuing theological development. His lectures included lectures on Hegel's philosophy, current theology in the early 20th century, as well as two of Bonhoeffer's most important theological works, *Creation and Fall* and the Christology lectures. In these lectures we see Bonhoeffer breaking new ground. First, with *Creation and Fall,*[10] Bonhoeffer ventures more deeply into the area of Biblical theology, offering what the subtitle of the published work called *A Theological Exposition of Genesis 1–3*.

While this piece was criticized by experts in the Hebrew Bible, we find an emphasis in Bonhoeffer that is quite different from both *Sanctorum Communio* and *Act and Being*. In those texts, we see Bonhoeffer doing primarily philosophical work, using theology for the sake of doing philosophy. In *Creation and Fall*, on the other hand, we find a sustained engagement with Scripture, marking a deepening of Bonhoeffer's attention on the revealed Word of God, an emphasis that he learned from Barth in the mid-1920s, but that he now begins to demonstrate more clearly in his own theology.

His Christology lectures represent another evolution in Bonhoeffer's theology: a more sustained Christocentrism in which his earlier focus on the community is not eclipsed, but through which his view of the community is more sharply focused. Jesus Christ gains a more central position in Bonhoeffer's theology, and also in his own life. Christ becomes the unifying vision for Bonhoeffer that would carry him through to the end of his life. In these lectures, he asserts that all of history and nature can only be viewed properly through the lens of Christ, who Bonhoeffer proposes is the center of human existence, the center of history, and the center between God and nature. In his latter days, Bonhoeffer will describe Jesus as the 'Man for Others'; in the early 1930s, the foundation for this assertion is laid.

After lecturing at Berlin for three years, Bonhoeffer once again traveled abroad, this time to pastor two German speaking churches in London.[11] Here, he was strategically placed to help Germans who were already beginning to flee Germany, and it was during this time that he became acquainted with Bishop George Bell of Chichester, a relationship that was to be of considerable importance for Bonhoeffer's later involvement with the conspiracy against Hitler. Bonhoeffer pastored in London for nearly 18 months, returning to Germany in the spring of 1935 to take his new vocation, leader of one of the five Confessing Church Preachers' Seminaries.

On the importance of this work to Bonhoeffer, Bethge writes, 'He had finally begun a work about which he had no reservations. In preceding years he had been haunted by the thought that he had not yet found his true task in life; now his new calling gave him the opportunity he longed for.'[12] This new calling was an opportunity for Bonhoeffer to live out what he had been thinking and writing about for nearly a decade: a true life together, living in community with brothers and sisters who were serious about loving God and each other, and were committed to the word of God. Later, in a circular letter to these seminarians written after the dissolution of the seminary, Bonhoeffer wrote, 'The matter of the proper education of preachers of the gospel is worthy of our ultimate commitment';[13] there is no doubt that in the following years, Bonhoeffer truly was ultimately committed, and that he went about this work with no reservations.

Out of his leading of the illegal seminary in Zingst and Finkenwalde come two of Bonhoeffer's most recognized works, *Life Together* and *Discipleship*. It would not be surprising if many of the readers of this present book began their studies of Bonhoeffer through one or both of these works. Both have been labeled as 'spiritual classics', and they maintain their appeal to readers up to this day. In these, we find Bonhoeffer's zeal for commitment to Christ and to the community in which He dwells. In many ways, these books sum up much of what Bonhoeffer had developed theologically up to that time: the emphasis on community that is found in *Sanctorum Communio* and *Act and Being* is combined with the Christology of the Berlin lectures, yielding two books full of richness and depth. These books arise out of the deep wells in Bonhoeffer's own journey, a time of deepening his own spiritual life and deepening community with his students at Finkenwalde, most notably with Eberhard Bethge.

The Finkenwalde seminary was closed by the Gestapo in September 1937. During 1938–1940, Bonhoeffer was involved in the collective pastorates of the Confessing Church, and traveling to England and America. This was a time of monumental decisions, and movement in his theology. Bonhoeffer had to decide the path he would take through the coming war. After spending a few weeks in America in 1939, Bonhoeffer famously decided that he could not be of any use in a post-war Germany were he to sit out the war on the sidelines. He returned to Germany, and, thus, to a deeper involvement in the conspiracy to which he was connected through his brother-in-law, Hans von Dohnanyi.

The years between his return to Germany and his arrest in 1943 were marked by a nomadic existence. For much of this time, Bonhoeffer's official residence was Munich, as he was posted there to accomplish his official duties as a member of the Military Intelligence office. However, he spent little time actually in Munich. Though he had been banned by the authorities from public meetings and speaking, he continued to spend considerable time in Berlin, meeting privately with members of the Confessing Church, and continuing to work to shore up the courage of those who would lead the battles against the Nazis.

An irony for Bonhoeffer was that war time provided him leisure for theological work, and he spent this time working on the project that had been on his heart and mind for quite some time. *Ethics* was, for Bonhoeffer, the work that he had wanted to write for many years.[14] Again, we see his passion for the Church and for Christ come together, this time in the form of a new vision of ethics that would challenge much of the history of ethical thought in the Western tradition. For Bonhoeffer, what mattered was not the question of what was the right thing to do, but what was the will of God.[15] Thinking that is isolated from this question becomes ethics that is not oriented to the center, Jesus Christ. It is ethics that removes one from the reality of the world instead of taking one deeply into the reality of the world.

Bonhoeffer's movement into the reality of the world led him to his involvement with a group of conspirators who desired an overthrow of Hitler's government and the establishment of a new government in Germany. Bonhoeffer's connection to this group was his brother-in-law, Hans von Dohnanyi, who was an officer in Germany's *Abwehr*, or counter-intelligence. Officially, Bonhoeffer was conscripted to be an officer in the *Abwehr*, but unofficially, he was a double agent who fed information about the plotters to the Allies using his connections from his time working with the ecumenical movement. Specifically, Bonhoeffer communicated the intentions and plans of the plotters to Bishop George Bell, who would pass the information on to the British government. In doing this, Bonhoeffer was committing treason against his country, and was involved in a plot that would commit tyranicide. In many ways, *Ethics* is the way that Bonhoeffer is thinking through and making sense of what he knew he had to do. To follow Jesus doesn't mean that we can avoid ambiguity and suffering, but in fact means that we must be willing to enter into deep ambiguity and suffering, which is certainly what Bonhoeffer did.

Ultimately, Bonhoeffer's work with the conspirators was discovered, and in spring of 1943, Bonhoeffer was arrested and sent to Tegel prison in Berlin. Here, he spent the bulk of the next two years of his life, reading, comforting his fellow prisoners, and thinking deeply about the future of Christianity in the post-war world. During this time, Bonhoeffer composed the letters that would become so important for his theological legacy. We find in these letters his thoughts regarding the need for Christianity to rethink itself, to understand more deeply its essence, and to be better equipped to engage with life in the 'world come of age'.

Unfortunately, Bonhoeffer was unable to bring his thoughts in the prison letters to fruition. After the failed attempt to assassinate Hitler on 20 July 1944, the Führer set his mind to eliminate all of his political enemies. Through a more thorough investigation, Bonhoeffer's connection to the conspirators was brought to light, therefore assuring his death. On 9 April, 1945, Bonhoeffer was hanged at the Flossenbürg concentration camp, ending his dramatic and all too short life.

THE APPROACH OF THIS BOOK

As we have walked through this brief introduction to Bonhoeffer's life, three themes have recurred: Christ, the Church, and the world. These are three fundamentals in Bonhoeffer, and they are fundamentals which will guide our study in this book. In looking to fundamentals, there are two opposite but equally risky dangers: first, assuming that they are *too* fundamental and thus ignoring them, supposing that they need not be mentioned because everyone knows them. This is the temptation of delving into the details without reference to the big picture, and therefore missing the forest for the trees. The second temptation is to become fundamentalist, adhering slavishly to the fundamentals without nuance. My desire in this book is to do neither of these, but to guide the reader into the details through a careful consideration of fundamentals. No doubt other Bonhoeffer scholars would state different fundamentals; I would have no quibble with them if they did. However, for the purposes of this book, these three themes will be our guides, and we will use them as entry points into the more perplexing nature of Bonhoeffer's theology.

My purpose in writing a 'guide for the perplexed' about Bonhoeffer is to enable readers to deepen their study of this important and intriguing theologian by increasing the readers' ability to see connections across Bonhoeffer's work. Bonhoeffer is one of the most quoted figures in the history of theology, and his name is everywhere these days. But what is too often lacking in those who would cite Bonhoeffer or would use him to support their particular point is a grasp of the context, both historical and theological, from which the quotes arise. Because of the nature of this theology and the fact that he died young before he had the opportunity to answer the questions he raised, one can make Bonhoeffer say just about anything one wants. There are plenty of sound bites available from the Bonhoeffer *corpus*. But in order to put ourselves in a better position to truly understand him, and thus to understand how to be spurred on by him as well as where to critique him, we must do the hard work of understanding both the big picture and the nuance of his theology. Karl Barth was correct when he wrote that Bonhoeffer was not a systematic thinker, and as such the threads that run through Bonhoeffer's theological tapestry can be difficult to discern. The aim of this book is to guide the reader who would think with, through, and beyond Bonhoeffer with a clearer view of the tapestry.

To do this, I begin by asking the following question: Would Dietrich Bonhoeffer be a perplexing figure in need of intensive study had the letters he wrote in prison never been smuggled out to his best friend? Would he have become such an important figure in theological studies had these letters perished with him? There is little doubt that the nature of Bonhoeffer's unfinished theological ruminations have made him a thinker whose influence has grown as theologians and pastors have continued to try to make sense of (and bring to fruition) the Bonhoeffer legacy.[16] To guide our ability to see connections across Bonhoeffer's work, this book will use the 'perplexing' themes of the prison letters as structural elements for engaging Bonhoeffer's larger theological project.

All too often, writers have *interpreted* Bonhoeffer from these letters, seeing them as discontinuous and thus overturning his earlier theology.[17] This is, in my view, an unfruitful approach to Bonhoeffer. Instead, I propose that each of the themes from the prison letters that we will investigate is best understood only from within the context of Bonhoeffer's larger theological project. Thus, for this guide, I am using five key themes from the prison letters as themes that will help us to see both the big picture and the nuances of Bonhoeffer's theology. My goal is to avoid the mistake that is always a temptation in reading Bonhoeffer: reading back from the letters as the hermeneutical key for approaching Bonhoeffer, thereby underplaying or denying the importance of the earlier works as movements culminating in the prison correspondence and not unnecessary precursors to the prison correspondence. As such, I will engage the perplexing statements of the prison letters in so far as they are contextualized by and emerge out of Bonhoeffer's theological project.

There is no doubt that there is development in Bonhoeffer's theology as it progresses through his life, and there can also be no doubt that he is pushing into some new territory with his thinking in the prison letters. However, our understanding of these statements and the territory to which they point can only be best understood when seen within the *oeuvre* of Bonhoeffer's theology. While this approach is not unique among Bonhoeffer scholars, it is important in a book such as this, which aims to be a guide for those furthering their study in Bonhoeffer. As such, I believe it is the best approach for a book that engages the difficulties in Bonhoeffer at something more than an introductory level, and yet will provide the reader with a greater understanding not only of the difficulties but of the breadth and depth of Bonhoeffer's theological vision.

The organization of the book will give each chapter a definite construction. I will begin with an overview of the theme from the prison letters that is under investigation in that chapter, consisting of a more general introduction and remarks on that theme. Following this, we will move backward into Bonhoeffer's earlier theology to show how the theme developed within the context of Bonhoeffer's theological movement. As such, we will have the opportunity to make a fresh pass through Bonhoeffer in each chapter, stopping at the key points along the way to which the theme of the chapter directs us.

The overall structure of the book is as follows: Chapters 2–4 set out what I suggest are the foundational themes in Bonhoeffer's theology: Christ, church, and world. Then, Chapters 5–6 pick up two further important themes from the prison letters: *Etsi deus non daretur*, living as if God were not given, through which we will attend to Bonhoeffer's conception of the weakness of God, and 'religionless Christianity', through which we will see Bonhoeffer's vision of a renewed Christianity in a world come of age. I will conclude the book in Chapter 7 by drawing together some of the various strands and suggesting some ways that Bonhoeffer's theological vision can be understood as we move forward in the 21st century.

CHAPTER 2

'WHO IS JESUS CHRIST FOR US TODAY?': THE CENTRALITY OF CHRIST IN BONHOEFFER'S THEOLOGY

In a letter written to Eberhard Bethge on 30 April 1944, Bonhoeffer writes, 'What is bothering me incessantly is the question what Christianity really is, or indeed who Christ really is, for us today?'[1] One can sense in this question something of a crystallizing moment for Bonhoeffer. His theological and personal journey, which have steered his course to a prison cell, can be summed up in the question 'Who is Jesus Christ for us today?' In this we see the importance of Jesus Christ for Bonhoeffer's theology, and it is with this central element that we begin our investigation of Bonhoeffer's thought.

The letter that contains this sentence is the first of the so-called 'theological letters' in which Bonhoeffer begins sketching out his thoughts on the way that theology would have to progress in the future that he envisions after the war. By this time, Bonhoeffer believes that Germany will lose the war, so he is casting his mind toward the uncertain future of his homeland, and indeed the West, following the trauma of World War II. The world has changed dramatically, and Bonhoeffer is thinking through the implications of these changes for the proclamation of Christ as Lord. At the heart of Bonhoeffer's question is the desire to explore the importance of Christ for the world *as it now stands*. Following the Enlightenment and the devastation of two world wars, humanity is no longer able to accept the metaphysical underpinnings of traditional Christianity, what Bonhoeffer calls 'the religious *a priori* of mankind'.[2] Bonhoeffer senses that the Western world is moving toward a 'religionless time' in which 'people as they are now simply cannot be religious any more'.[3]

Because of this new historical setting, the question that he asks is centered on the person of Christ and his encounter with *these* humans. How is Christ to be understood in this context by these people?

Bonhoeffer is clear about the question that he is asking when exploring the place of Christ in this new world: 'How can Christ become Lord of the religionless as well?'[4] Bonhoeffer is not interested in redefining the lordship of Christ in the new 'religionless' setting but to explore how he is present and engaged as Lord in this new historical setting. Bonhoeffer's project is to proclaim and live out the Lordship of Christ as a concept that is 'religionless', i.e., not based on certain foundations that have sustained Western Christianity for her 2,000-year history. In other words, what Bonhoeffer desires to accomplish in the prison letters is a fundamental rethinking of *Christianity*, but not a fundamental rethinking of *Christ*. For Bonhoeffer, the question is not a question whether or not Christ is Lord of the world, but a question of *how this Lordship is to be pronounced and lived out in the new world setting* of 'the world come of age'. We will discuss the concept of the world come of age more carefully later on; our attention at this point is on the centrality of Christ in Bonhoeffer's theology, a theme that must be understood before we can make connections to Bonhoeffer's other theological themes.

We will now cast our gaze backward over Bonhoeffer's theological career to explore the place of Jesus Christ in his theology. Bonhoeffer suggests that Christ is the center of reality, and as such it only makes sense that Christ would be at the center of Bonhoeffer's theology. It is to a full view of this centrality that we now turn.

CHRISTOLOGY IN *SANCTORUM COMMUNIO* AND *ACT AND BEING*

As has been indicated, this book will approach Bonhoeffer's theological foundations from the perspective of three core themes: Christ, church, and world. Because of the key function that Christology plays in Bonhoeffer's theology, we are beginning with it. However, in turning our attention to Bonhoeffer's earlier theology, we will find there a significant emphasis on the church, and a view to Christ insofar as He is in relation to this community. The question could be raised: why not, then, begin with ecclesiology? I have not chosen this approach because of the weight that Christology bears in Bonhoeffer's theology. This does not mean, of course, that we can neatly separate Christ and church in

Bonhoeffer's earliest theological works. My view in this chapter, however, will be toward the Christological themes, and then we will turn in the next chapter to view the ecclesial themes more closely.

The importance of Christ is evidenced in Bonhoeffer's earliest writings. Even as a student, Bonhoeffer was thinking deeply about the person and function of Christ. But it is in his doctoral dissertation, *Sanctorum Communio*, that we find Bonhoeffer's thoughts about the centrality of Christ taking definite shape. Although *Sanctorum Communio* is a work that seeks to explore the sociological and theological nature of the church, one cannot but recognize the central role that Christ plays in this work. In his dissertation, Bonhoeffer engages with an issue that was drawing the attention of many theologians in the 1920s: the question of the nature of the community of faith. Bonhoeffer's approach in *Sanctorum Communio* is to engage this question through a dialogue with sociological and theological insights into the nature of the church. His fundamental argument is that church is a community that can be analyzed from outside through sociological analysis, but that one cannot truly grasp the nature of the church apart from an understanding of the church as the revelation of God, a community in whom the life of God dwells and in whom the form of Christ is being formed.

Bonhoeffer begins *Sanctorum Communio* by stating his methodological approach. His purpose is 'to understand the structure of the given reality of a church of Christ, as revealed in Christ, from the perspective of social philosophy and sociology'.[5] As such, Bonhoeffer will use the tools available to him from the fields of the social sciences to investigate the church community. However, we have to be careful to grasp Bonhoeffer's intent: he is not investigating the church as a philosopher or social scientist. Instead, his desire is to appropriate the findings of social philosophy and sociology in order to approach his study of the church from a distinctly theological perspective. He writes, '[I]t should be noted that this study of the sanctorum communio does not properly belong to the sociology of religion, but to theology. It will be carried out on the foundation of Christian theology and will make fruitful for theology the fundamental insights that derive from social philosophy and sociology.'[6] This is clear in the subtitle of the work, 'A Theological Study of the Sociology of the Church'. Bonhoeffer will lay out a sociology of the church, but is quite clear that the insights of sociology cannot themselves adequately grasp the nature of Christian community. Instead, 'the nature of the church can only be understood from within, *cum ira et studio*, never by nonparticipants. Only those who take the claim of the church seriously . . . can possibly glimpse something of its true nature'.[7] So, Bonhoeffer is focusing on the sociality of the church, but is doing so from the perspective of faith. It is somewhat misleading when Bonhoeffer says he is looking at the church from the perspective of social philosophy and sociology because it is clear in his methodological approach that only faith can truly grasp the nature of the community.

In turning to the body of the book, Bonhoeffer begins by laying out what Clifford Green refers to as a 'programmatic' aspect of Bonhoeffer's theology: the communal nature of Christian concepts.[8] In particular, Bonhoeffer approaches the Christian notion of personhood as something that must be understood as a social concept, and which is intertwined with one's understanding of God.[9] God, community, and personhood cannot be developed apart from one another, and this sets a Christian concept of person apart from other philosophical or sociological conceptions of persons, or of 'social basic-relations'.[10] Social basic-relations are the fundamental assumptions about humans and human relationality that are used by various fields of study. Bonhoeffer asserts that neither philosophical or sociological social basic-relations yield an understanding of personhood that can grasp the nature of the church, exactly because none of them defines person as a social term. Personhood is defined through individuality in each of these systems, though, of course, each has a different way of asserting that individuality.

What makes the Christian concept of person unique, however, is that in Christian theology person is a communal concept. Bonhoeffer describes the way in which the Biblical narrative emphasizes the importance of communality for understanding God and humanity. He asserts the Christian conception of personhood in contrast to the idealistic conception of personhood, which asserts the absoluteness of the individual, and therefore cannot conceive of the notion of person as *essentially* communal. In contrast to this, the Christian notion recognizes that only God can be called 'absolute', and as such the human person is only truly person in relation to God.[11] To be person *is* to be in relation to the other, both to God who is the creator and thus giver of personhood, as well as to other humans. It is only in being confronted by the other that the human individual can be a person, and so it is only as a community of individuals who confront one another that humanity is human. As such, it is only as 'collective persons' that humans are human. Individuals are only truly individuals insofar as they are confronted and given personhood by others. Bonhoeffer's succinct statement of this theological tenet is as follows: '. . . for the individual to exist, "others" must necessarily be there'.[12] However, it is not the neighbor who we ultimately encounter in our relationships with others. Instead, we are encountered by Christ in the neighbor. God has created humanity to be creatures who exist in sociality, and it is he, in the person of Jesus Christ, who is the ultimate You who confronts humanity.[13]

To understand the importance of Christ in Bonhoeffer's early theology, we must unpack the notion of collective persons to which we just referred. Because humanity *is* only in relationship with others, the persons to whom we are related are definitive of what we are. In *Act and Being*, Bonhoeffer states that people receive their identity from the social group to which they belong, beginning with immediate families, and moving more broadly to extended family units, communities, regions, and nations. However, theologically speaking, we cannot understand humanity simply from their relation to other humans or national groupings, but must instead understand humanity as theologically related to one of two heads: Adam or Christ.[14] As such, all humanity exists either *in Adam* or *in Christ*. In the most foundational sense, one's being is determined by relationship either to Adam or to Christ. Adam is the collective person of the old humanity, while Christ is the collective person of the new. The implication of this for the community is that the church *is* the Body of Christ. To understand the importance of this for both Bonhoeffer's Christology and his ecclesiology, this must be taken as more than a mere word picture, more than a metaphor: Bonhoeffer believes strongly in the presence of Christ through the actualizing work of the Spirit, a dynamic that understands the church to be, in Bonhoeffer's famous dictum, 'Christ existing as community'. We will spend the rest of this section exploring what Bonhoeffer means by this phrase.

'Christ existing as community' is Bonhoeffer's way of expressing the ontology of the church community. In both *Sanctorum Communio* and *Act and Being*, Bonhoeffer is interested in the revelatory significance of the church. Especially in *Act and Being*, Bonhoeffer challenges various proposals for understanding the ontological status of divine revelation, engaging with various understandings of how God has revealed himself and how that revelation takes form in history. Specifically, Bonhoeffer critiques the actualism of Karl Barth, in which Barth denies any permanence of divine revelation in history, as well as Roman Catholic institutionalism and neo-scholastic Biblicism, in which revelation, in the former, is seen as being contained in the hierarchy of the church and, in the latter, is contained in the Bible. Bonhoeffer wants to find a different option than any of these for locating the presence of revelation in history, and he does so through his notion of 'Christ existing as community'.

To grasp Bonhoeffer's counter proposal, we must take a moment to understand his conversation partner, Karl Barth. In Barth's early theology, he rejects the liberal theological teaching, especially espoused by Friedrich Schleiermacher, that asserts an innate connection to God in all human persons. For Schleiermacher, the religious *a priori* consists in a universal 'feeling of absolute dependence'. To connect with God, one must do so by connecting with this universal feeling. While the details of Schleiermacher's proposal are not important here, Barth's critique of its effect is: for Barth, Scheiermacher makes relationship to God an immanent feature of human existence, thereby ultimately capturing God within human being. In other words, the critical component of Barth's critique of liberalism is that it denies God's freedom to be God, and most importantly, it denies the freedom of God's Word to come to the human from outside. The danger in Schleiermacher's theology is that the Word of God is no longer foreign, no longer alien, but becomes an aspect of human conscience. Barth, on the other hand, wants to restore the Reformation emphasis on the Word of God as that which comes as an alien and saving Word from outside the human.

In order to stress this point, Barth strongly emphasizes the freedom of God over against humanity. His Word comes to the world from outside the world, and cannot in any way be conceived as immanent within the world. This is what is known as Barth's actualism: the Word of God is always act, always event. The Word can never take form as being, because to assert that the Word of God has being (either being in the consciousness of humanity or in the Bible) is to assert that it has lost its freedom as a living Word and has instead become a dead letter. Barth's insistence on the actualism of the Word creates two related problems: first, if God's Word is only event, and thus has no being in the world, how can one understand Jesus Christ? Second, if God's Word doesn't take form in history, then is there any consistency between one experience of God's Word and the next? Is every new encounter with the Word a new encounter, or is there any way to speak of a consistency of encounter with God?

Bonhoeffer appreciates Barth's emphasis on divine freedom over against all human attempts to pin God down and thus press him into the service of whatever ideology needs his support. But he doesn't feel that Barth's actualism pays enough attention to the actual entry of God into history through the incarnation. Barth describes a God who touches history from outside but seems to not truly enter history. But, if one takes seriously that Christ is the presence of God on earth in the incarnation, then this must have dramatic effects on one's understanding of revelation. In Bonhoeffer's judgment, Barth has failed to do just that. In *Act and Being*, Bonhoeffer counters Barth's concept of the freedom of God when he famously writes, 'God *is* present, that is, not in eternal non-objectivity but – to put it quite provisionally for now – "haveable", graspable in the Word within the church'.[15] Bonhoeffer is saying that Barth is right to assert divine freedom, but he is wrong to assert that God's freedom consists in God being free *from* humans. Instead, Bonhoeffer insists, God's freedom is a freedom *for* us, and he has chosen the manner in which he would be free for us: the incarnation of Christ and God's true entry into history as one of us.

Because of this, Bonhoeffer stresses the centrality of Christ in his theology in ways that Barth would only come to later. 'Christ existing as community' is the way that Bonhoeffer brings together Christ, the church, and the revelation of God. For him, God entered into history in the person of Jesus Christ, and he continues to be in history through the presence of Christ in the church. Christ is the revelation of God, and because he is the form of the church, the church is now a revelatory event. The church is not simply a community that gathers to read God's written revelation; no, the church *is* God's revelation of humanity reconciled to God and neighbor, a community that understands God's work in history to restore the human creature to God's intention of human sociality. So, the church community is the presence of Christ in history through the mediating work of the Spirit, and therefore is the place of God's revelation in history. Bonhoeffer writes:

> [Revelation] must . . . be thought in the church, for the church is the present Christ, 'Christ existing as community'. . . . Christ is the corporate person of the Christian community of faith. . . . For this

> reason, the Protestant idea of the church is conceived in personal terms – that is, God reveals the divine self in the church as person. The community of faith is God's final revelation as 'Christ existing as community,' ordained for the end time of the world until the return of Christ.[16]

The church is the concrete, historical community wherein Christ's new humanity is being formed and dwells. Therefore, the church is 'Christ existing as community'.

To summarize our thoughts on Bonhoeffer's early theology and the Christology contained therein: Bonhoeffer begins his theological reflections by focusing on the church, the community that is the place of God's ongoing historical engagement with the world through which He is revealing his plan for humanity. However, the ontological foundation of the church is Jesus Christ, and as such we see his centrality to Bonhoeffer's reflections on the *Sanctorum Communio*. 'Christ existing as community' is the crystallizing concept through which Bonhoeffer's commitment to the centrality of Christ for understanding the church can be seen.

Having demonstrated Bonhoeffer's early focus on Christ through his discussions in *Sanctorum Communio* and *Act and Being* regarding the presence of Christ in the church as the mode of divine revelation, we can now turn to the text which is critical for seeing how Bonhoeffer's Christology develops methodologically, his series of lectures on Christology from 1933, as well as his lectures on Genesis 1–3, published as *Creation and Fall.*

THE CHRISTOLOGY LECTURES AND *CREATION AND FALL*

In the summer of 1933, Bonhoeffer presented a series of lectures on Christology. Outside of the walls of the lecture room at the University of Berlin, the Nazis were solidifying their grip on the government. Hitler was being hailed as the Germanic Messiah who would lead Germany to resurrection, overcoming the shame of the Versailles Treaty that ended World War I, a treaty that declared the Germans to be completely at fault for the war. Inside the walls of the lecture room, Bonhoeffer declared that Jesus Christ is the Messiah, and no other can take his place.[17] In these lectures, Bonhoeffer is laying out the ground work of his resistance to Nazism by concentrating on the place of God's revelation, Jesus Christ. In contrast to this, the Nazis are proclaiming the 'orders of creation', an ideology which proclaims that God reveals his will not simply in Scripture or through Jesus Christ, but through the means of *Volk*, race, and the nation. In other words, one of the critical questions at the heart of Bonhoeffer's resistance to the Nazis is the question of the Lordship of Christ and his relation to the ideologies of humanity. In the last section, we explored Bonhoeffer's understanding of divine revelation as centered in Christ as he exists in the community of the church. As we turn to the Christology lectures we see Bonhoeffer continue to develop his commitment to the centrality of Christ. He is the Lord who has claimed the world, and no other can claim authority over him, not a people, not a race, not a nation, and not a dictator.

In the Christology lectures, Bonhoeffer is fundamentally laying out his epistemology. Christ is described in these lectures as 'the Counter-Logos', while human reason is 'the logos'. Christ is the one who comes to the human person and challenges her claim to know truth. With this comes an attack on the human pretension to be able to know all things apart from God's revelation of himself. For Bonhoeffer, there is certainly a realm in which human knowledge is capable of knowing truth, but it is only through the coming of Christ that the logos is countered with a Truth that it cannot grasp on its own.

In order to analyze the shape of the Christology lectures, and especially the rubric of 'logos/Counter-Logos', we need to comprehend Bonhoeffer's theology of sin.[18] Bonhoeffer adopts Luther's notion of sin as the *cor curvum in se*, 'the heart turned in on itself'. As we have seen, the human was created by God to be a social being, and in fact, we can only understand what it means to be human by stressing that the Christian conception of personhood is a social concept. To understand human sin, then, is to understand it as the destruction of human sociality. Through sin, the human who was created to live in loving fellowship with God and neighbor becomes turned in on the self, oriented toward the self as the highest good instead of directed outward in love of God and neighbor. Sin takes the human from being in relationship to others through self-giving and respecting the other as my boundary, to self-love that no longer respects the other but, in fact, despises the other. The person who is my boundary is no longer seen as one to love, but now is seen as my competitor. The heart that was created to be oriented outward, toward others, is now the *cor curvum in se*, the heart that has the self as its highest object.

The implications of this are many. For our present purposes, we will focus on how Bonhoeffer's conception of sin affects his epistemology, and how we can see the centrality of Christ to Bonhoeffer's understanding of human knowing and thus human existence. In *Act and Being*, Bonhoeffer critiques idealist philosophical epistemology through an analysis of the effects of the *cor curvum in se* on human reason. His critique is simple: idealist philosophy doesn't recognize that human beings are unable to place themselves into truth exactly because they deny the reality of human sin. Because of this, for humans to be freed from their condition of being turned in on the self they must be placed into truth from outside. The *cor curvum in se* cannot reach outside the self and truly find the truth that transcends human subjectivity.

We can only understand Bonhoeffer's claim here if we grasp that, for him, transcendence is not a metaphysical concept but an ethical one. Transcendence is not about God being 'out there' but about the person who transcends us and thus sets up an ethical demand on us. In other words, transcendence is related to the conception of being bounded by others. This notion of transcendence is intertwined with Bonhoeffer's notion of sin: sin is to fail to recognize and respect the other who transcends me. Idealist philosophy fails because it views transcendence in terms of ideas instead of persons. Idealism believes in the ability of the rational mind to set itself into truth through ideas instead of recognizing that truth is about personal interaction. It is in the Christology lectures that we see Bonhoeffer work out more fully this notion of encounter and being placed into truth as a theologico-epistemological concept.

Bonhoeffer does this through the rubric of 'logos and Counter-Logos'. Although the Biblical testimony refers to Christ as Logos, Bonhoeffer uses this referent for humanity and its confidence in its own ability to know the truth through the categorizing use of reason. The human logos is constantly seeking to know truth through its ability to categorize the world around it and thus make sense of the world. In other words, the human mind seeks scientific classification in order to know and in order to assert its control over history. This means that the human mind is constantly asking two questions: 'What is the cause of X?' and 'What is the meaning of X?', both of which are questions of classification.[19] At base, all scientific, classifying questions are asking the question 'how?' or 'what?'. But what about the claim of Christ to be Lord? The logos will raise the same questions of Christ: 'How is such a claim possible?'[20] The logos continues on in its goal of classifying all knowledge through approaching the claims of Christ with the scientific questions of 'what?' and 'how?'. The problem with this, according to Bonhoeffer, is that one can never come to understand who Christ is by asking the questions of immanent human reason. Christ is not bound by the questions 'how?' and 'what?'. Bonhoeffer sets up the problem through a string of questions that Christ raises for the human logos. He asks, 'What happens when doubt is thrown upon the presupposition of his scientific activity? What happens if somewhere the claim is raised that the human logos is superseded, condemned, dead? What happens if a Counter-Logos appears which denies classification? Another logos which destroys the first?'[21] This, says Bonhoeffer, is exactly what happens in the incarnation of Jesus Christ. One has appeared within the realm of human history and rationality who does not fit into the categorization of immanent human reason. This one, Jesus Christ, claims that he is the Messiah who cannot be classified as one object of knowledge among the many that are available to the human mind. Instead of being an idea, this one is the Word 'who challenges the dominion of the logos'.[22] The appearance of Christ relativizes the human mind, thereby showing the human mind that it is incapable of classifying the Word that is a person and not an idea. An idea can be classified; the Person of Jesus cannot. This leaves the logos in a state of confusion. If the normal questions do not apply, then what can the mind do? Bonhoeffer suggests that there is one question left that is the only proper question to ask the Counter-Logos: 'who are you?' He writes, 'The question, "Who are you?", is the question of dethroned and distraught reason; but it is also the question of faith: "Who are you? Are you God Himself?" This is the question with which Christology is concerned'.[23]

Bonhoeffer here makes the connection between the 'who' question and transcendence. We recall that Bonhoeffer conceives of transcendence as an ethical and not a metaphysical concept. The personalist account of transcendence is brought to a point: only when we ask the question 'who' do we recognize Christ's transcendent encounter of the human that calls us to be placed into truth, i.e., that demands faith and opens up reconciliation with God. The 'how' question is a question of immanence and is a question of the *cor curvum in se* that desires to know the truth through its own resources. But in asking 'who are you?', the human relinquishes her claim to be able to categorize Christ, and instead recognizes the claim that his appearance puts on the human. In the coming of the Counter-Logos, the logos is again confronted from the outside by the transcendent other who is its boundary, and thus is placed into truth and made aware of the grace of limitation.

We find in the rubric of the 'logos/Counter-Logos' another key feature for understanding Bonhoeffer's commitment to the centrality of Christ in his theology. Methodologically, Bonhoeffer makes an interesting move in these lectures: he begins with the present Christ and only then moves to the historical Christ. Bonhoeffer does not travel the road of many Christologies, which seek to establish the historicity of Christ before moving to the implications of the resurrection of Christ, if they ever do so.[24] But Bonhoeffer begins by asserting the presence of the Counter-Logos as the only proper place for beginning Christology. To begin with the Christ of history is to avoid the 'Who' that is the present Christ. To do Christology as history is to once again seek to categorize Christ. The present Christ is the presupposition apart from which there can be no Christology.[25] This conception of the present Christ is central to the later question that gives this chapter its theme: 'Who is Jesus Christ, for us, today?' For Bonhoeffer, Christology is not a historical discipline. The historical Christ is not unimportant, but what is of greater interest to Bonhoeffer is the present Christ. This is the question that he will carry with him through his life to the prison letters.

Beyond his statement that Christ is present, Bonhoeffer asserts that the present Christ has a particular structure: he is *Christus pro me*, Christ for me, another key feature of Bonhoeffer's Christology that carries with him to the end of his life, where, in the prison letters, Christ is defined as 'the Man for Others'. This *pro me* structure means that Christ cannot be thought of apart from his relationship to humanity. And, his presence to humanity takes on a particular definition: Christ is present as the hidden one. He is not present for all to see, but is present 'in the likeness of sinful flesh'.[26] Bonhoeffer is sure to stress: the humiliation of Christ is not that God becomes human, but that God truly takes on the sinful flesh of humanity; this is the scandal of the gospel. As the humiliated God-man, Christ goes to the cross, truly bearing in his flesh the sin which all humanity carries. The revelation of God in Christ is a revelation that isn't available to the logos, but is known to those who would recognize in faith the presence of Christ and be willing to ask: 'who are you'? We will see the influence of Christ's witness, and particularly the importance of the cross for Christ, as we move forward in this study.

Bonhoeffer's account of Christ and the demand that he places on the human logos demonstrates his methodological commitment to revelation that is centered on God's self-giving in Christ. The human mind cannot transcend itself and come to know the truth through the immanence of human reason. This is consistent with Bonhoeffer's earlier theology in *Sanctorum Communio* and *Act and Being*, where he indicates that the human doesn't find the truth but must be placed into truth through being in relation to Christ. We can see in the Christology lectures an emphasis on Christ that demonstrates his methodological commitment to Christ. What we will see as we move through his theology on our way back to the prison letters is a deepening commitment to the person of Christ, not merely as a theological method, but as the center of human existence and history.

Before we move on to *Discipleship*, we need to take a brief look at *Creation and Fall*. In this text, we see many of the themes that we have already become familiar with: the nature of human boundaries, sin as a fall into the self and therefore a loss of true communion, which is a loss of others, and the stress on the human as an ethical being who loses her bearings through the rejection of God. What is of interest to us in this chapter is not a full investigation of *Creation and Fall*, but a look at the end of the text, where we can see Bonhoeffer's focus on Christ becoming clearer.

To end the book, Bonhoeffer writes a beautiful meditation on the centrality of the cross as the end of the story told in Genesis 1–3. This ending may be surprising, but in *Creation and Fall* Bonhoeffer speaks of our knowledge of the beginning of history as only being understood from the end. The reason for this comes out of Bonhoeffer's continuing focus on the human need for revelation. Humanity cannot know the beginning of human history from the middle, where we find ourselves. Instead, it is only by knowing the end of the story, the resurrection of Christ, that we can have access to the beginning. In other words, Genesis is not a 'history' text that tells straight history that is available to unaided human reason. It is a revealed text that is open to the eyes of faith. The key to understanding the beginning of the story is to read it through the end of the story, the resurrection of Christ. It is only by knowing the resurrection of Christ that one is opened up to the revelation of the beginning of history in Genesis.[27]

At the end of *Creation and Fall*, Bonhoeffer speaks of Christ's work to restore humanity to the purpose intended by God in creation that was lost through Adam and Eve's rebellion. He writes,

> The end of Cain's history, and so the end of all history, is Christ on the cross, the murdered son of God. That is the last desperate assault on the gate of paradise. And under the whirling sword, under the cross, the human race dies. But Christ lives. The trunk of the cross becomes the wood of life, and now in the midst of the world, on the accursed ground itself, life is raised up anew. In the center of the world, from the wood of the cross, the fountain of life springs up. All who thirst for life are called to drink from this water, and whoever has eaten from the wood of this life shall never again hunger and thirst. What a strange paradise is this hill of Golgotha, this cross, this blood, this broken body. What a strange tree of life, this trunk on which the very God had to suffer and die. Yet it is the very kingdom of life and of the resurrection, which by grace God grants us again. It is the gate of imperishable hope now opened, the gate of waiting and of patience. The tree of life, the cross of Christ, the center of God's world that is fallen but upheld and preserved – that is what the end of the story about paradise is for us.[28]

In this paragraph, Bonhoeffer describes the centrality of Christ for human history. Note at the beginning his statement that the death of Christ is the end of history. Christ's history contains and sums up all human history. It is in him that life is renewed on earth, and the human history finds its destiny. *Creation and Fall*, though a book that explores the first few chapters of Genesis, is through and through a book about Jesus. In writing such a book, Bonhoeffer strengthens his commitment to the centrality of Christ.

We see in Bonhoeffer's days as a teacher in Berlin a deepening commitment to the centrality of Christ. During these days, Germany was entering into the national nightmare that was the Nazi reign. The days ahead of Bonhoeffer would take a further commitment to the centrality of Christ, and a deepening faith in his hidden presence in the darkest of days. In his famous work, *Discipleship*, we see Bonhoeffer straining to understand the disciple's task of following Christ, even through the valley of the shadow of death.

CHRIST AND *DISCIPLESHIP*

Discipleship is perhaps the most famous of Bonhoeffer's works. This text has been popularized (and almost canonized) in certain circles of the church, and this popularization has led to a mass reading of *Discipleship*, earning it a reputation as a spiritual classic. But one must be careful in interpreting *Discipleship*: it was not written to be a 'spiritual classic' but to be a meditation on following after Christ in the particular context of Nazi Germany in the 1930s. This doesn't mean that the book has no appeal to those living in a different time and different place, but it does mean that we cannot approach the book with a lack of awareness of its historical context.

Discipleship was a book that was long in the making. The book is constructed around an engagement with the Sermon on the Mount, a text that Bonhoeffer had been studying since his encounter with the French pacifist Jean Lasserre in New York during his year at Union Seminary. When he became the head of the illegal preachers' seminary in Finkenwalde, Bonhoeffer had the perfect opportunity both to teach and to live out Jesus' teachings in the sermon. *Discipleship* was largely composed during this time and as a reflection on the call of Christ to 'follow me'. The foundation of *Discipleship* is found in the methodology of the Christology lectures: the present Christ who encountered his disciples in the form of his flesh continues to encounter humanity today. The book is organized around the presence of Christ who calls people to follow him: the first half analyzes Christ's call to his disciples, and the second half is a discussion of how that call continues to be heard throughout history. What we have in this book is not a methodological working out of the centrality of Christ in purely theological terms, but an examination of Christ's existential encounter with his followers, and the demand that his call places on those who would become his disciples. In this we must consider clearly the historical setting of the book: Bonhoeffer was calling himself, his students at Finkenwalde, and the Confessing Church to a deeper commitment to following the living Christ to unexpected places in a deeply troubled and confusing time. *Discipleship* is Bonhoeffer's clarion call for the church to pay attention to Christ and to follow where he leads, thereby giving up her preconceived principles about the call of Christ in order to truly follow him.

We can see this focus on the call of Christ most clearly in chapter two, 'The Call to Discipleship'. Bonhoeffer begins this chapter with a meditation on Mark 2:14, which says 'As Jesus was walking along, he saw Levi son of Alphaeus sitting at the tax booth, and he said to him, "Follow me." And he got up and followed him.'[29] The suddenness of the call, and the immediate reaction, both offend our natural reason. We would expect a time of trial, a warming up period, an audition. Surely a sane person would never simply leave their job and follow after someone else the first time they are called! But such is the call of Christ: it is a call that demands, that offends, and that is costly. Bonhoeffer famously describes the difference between cheap grace and costly grace in the first chapter of the book. Cheap grace is grace as a principle, grace we give to ourselves. Costly grace is grace that places demands on the follower of Christ, grace that calls the follower to bear the cross. Ultimately, says Bonhoeffer, 'It is costly, because it calls to discipleship; it is grace, because it calls us to follow *Jesus Christ*. . . . Above all, grace is costly because it was costly to God, because it cost God the life of God's son . . . and because nothing can be cheap to us which is costly to God.'[30]

The costliness of grace means that we should not be surprised at the suddenness of the call to Levi, nor of his response. The costly grace of God in following after Christ is not one that accords with human reason: it comes as sheer demand and offer that arises from the authority of Christ.[31] He alone can make such a demand, and it is because the call comes from him that Levi leaves his tax booth and follows after Christ. Not only is Jesus the one who calls, he is the content of the call. There is no promise of what the path will hold for the disciple except that it consists of following after Christ. He is the content of discipleship. In obeying the call, the disciple has no promise of where the path will take her; what she has is the presence of Christ whom she is following. The call to discipleship means 'nothing other than being bound to Jesus Christ alone'.[32] The centrality of Christ that Bonhoeffer worked out methodologically in his earlier theology now bears fruit in a dedication to following after the present Christ who is the content of discipleship.

Though the content of discipleship is Christ himself, there is a further definition of the call to follow Christ: it is a call to bear the cross. *Discipleship* focuses attentively on the cruciform life. This is unsurprising as we again reflect on the context in which the book was written. Bonhoeffer is leading a group of seminarians who will inevitably face great suffering and many challenges to disown Christ for the sake of ease. By joining the Confessing Church, these students have removed themselves from the security of the state church, and are therefore not guaranteed a ministry position or a salary. Beyond this, there will inevitably be even more costly sacrifices ahead: sacrifices of family, of contentment, and, perhaps, of one's life. They had chosen a costly road, and Bonhoeffer here affirms the costliness through a concentration on the cross of Christ.

Christ's way leads to the cross, the place of selflessness, the place of death for others, the place of suffering. When Jesus calls his disciples to himself, he gives them a clear picture of where they will go: 'If anyone wants to become my followers, let them deny themselves and take up their cross and follow me.'[33] The call to follow is a call to cross bearing and suffering. Jesus himself will suffer, and so, therefore, will any who are his followers. Bonhoeffer asserts, 'Just as Christ is only Christ as one who suffers and is rejected, so a disciple is a disciple only in suffering and being rejected, thereby participating in crucifixion. Discipleship as allegiance to the person of Jesus Christ places the follower . . . under the cross.'[34] Bonhoeffer's intent here is clear: to follow Christ is to be led into suffering, and there is going to be much suffering for the church in the years to come. Bonhoeffer has foreseen as early as Hitler's rise to power that this would lead to war, and he is preparing his students for the suffering that will come as they seek to be faithful to the way of Christ.

But there is more going on here than merely propping up his students for tough times. There is a deeply theological point that Bonhoeffer is making. We have seen in our earlier exploration of the centrality of Christ in this chapter that Bonhoeffer conceives of human existence as existence for others, and this chapter is showing the way that Bonhoeffer's theology leads to his final definition of Christ as 'the Man for Others'. The cross is central to Bonhoeffer's vision of Christ as the Man for Others. It is at the cross that Jesus reveals the nature of his mission: at the cross, we see the God-man who exists for others taking on the nature of the *cor curvum in se* in order to overcome human selfishness and free humanity to life with God and one another in self-giving love. When Bonhoeffer focuses his attention on the cross in *Discipleship* he does not do so out of a morbid fascination with guilt and death, but with the theological conviction that it is in the place of Christ's great agony and suffering that we see the doorway to life. The cross is not an end in itself but is the means to and end: life for others. The cross is the means by which the old self, the *cor curvum in se*, is put to death through encounter with Christ. We see the positive nature with which Bonhoeffer views the cross in the following statement: 'The cross is not the terrible end of a pious, happy life. Instead, it stands at the beginning of community with Jesus Christ.'[35] The call to the cross is a call to death, but the call to death is a call to new life that is marked by forgiveness of sin and so freedom from self. The community of those who would follow after Christ is, fundamentally, a community of forgiveness. Those who know the forgiveness of the cross must themselves be persons who forgive. As such, Bonhoeffer can call the discipleship community, the Church, 'the community of forgiveness of sins'.[36]

As has been indicated, Bonhoeffer is not interested in simply recounting the call of Christ to his original followers but desires to express how this call continues to go forth in history. He ponders why the call to discipleship that is so prevalent in the Gospels is rarely discussed in Paul's letters. Bonhoeffer proposes that later in the New Testament the call to discipleship is replaced by an emphasis on baptism.[37] Baptism becomes a symbol of the call to the cross, for baptism is, in fact, a symbol of the followers union with the death (and resurrection) of Christ. For present day followers, we hear the call of Christ to follow him in the call to be baptized. Baptism is the response of the disciple to follow, just as Levi's response was to leave his tax booth and follow after Christ. Baptism initiates the follower into a life for others, a life of death that frees the self from the self in order to live ex-centric lives. The one who is baptized, and who remembers that baptism through daily dying with Christ through the sacraments, is one who is being set free for life with others. The concept of the cross, and its relation to baptism, is tied together to the ethical conceptions that we have seen throughout our study of Bonhoeffer's early Christology: Christ is the one who lives for others as an ethical self, and those who follow Christ are those who follow in this path, a path that leads to suffering and death of the old self as the doorway to the life of the new self. *Discipleship*, then, is thoroughly christological, and therefore intrinsically ethical.

As we have seen, Bonhoeffer's focus in *Discipleship* is on the existential encounter of the disciple with Christ. The historical location of the writing is important for understanding Bonhoeffer's concentrated focus on following Christ into suffering, and the emphasis on the costly grace of the gospel. Bonhoeffer knew the need of the day, and stressed the need for the church to be faithful to the Lordship of Christ and his call to suffering.

CHRIST AND *ETHICS*

The seminary at Finkenwalde was closed by the Gestapo in 1937, effectively leaving Bonhoeffer without a ministry. He continued to work with the Confessing Church training pastors through the collective pastorates, but he was no longer able to pour his energies into life together with his seminarians. Instead, Bonhoeffer's energies would be channeled to writing the book that he had long desired to write, *Ethics*. Bonhoeffer never completed *Ethics*. What we have is a collection of essays which are the basis for chapters that were to eventually be worked into the final form of the book. But what we do have in *Ethics* is a continuing development of Bonhoeffer's Christology, and a clearer picture of the nature of Christ and the ethical implications of following him. The attention of this section will be on the place of Christ in *Ethics*, seeing the way that the Christology of *Ethics* both flows from and expands Bonhoeffer's earlier Christology. This analysis will put us in position to close this chapter with some final reflections on Bonhoeffer's definition of Christ in the prison letters.

At the center of our discussion of the Christology of *Ethics* is Bonhoeffer's conception of *Stellvertretung*, or 'vicarious representative action'. This notion is critical to Bonhoeffer's understanding of the person and function of Jesus Christ. We have seen throughout this chapter that Bonhoeffer defines Jesus as the Man for Others. In *Ethics*, he describes 'the Structure of the Responsible Life', outlining a conception of the ethical life that centers on living for others and not on rules and principles.[38] To be ethical is not to live by certain rules, but to live a responsible life for others. For Bonhoeffer, Jesus Christ defines this vision, and so defines for humanity what it means to live ethically. His understanding of Jesus as the one who lives the responsible life can best be understood through an analysis of the notion of 'vicarious representative action'.

For Bonhoeffer, vicarious representation is the life of responsibility that is the life of freedom. To be for others is to be free from self. To be a responsible ethical agent means that one has recognized the other and has given oneself for the sake of the other. What we see in the life of Jesus Christ is the freedom par excellence that God has given to humanity. In order for humans to live freely, they must make the ethical decision to be for others through living responsible lives. In other words, 'freedom exhibits itself in *my accountability* for my living and acting, and in the *venture* of concrete decision. This, then, is the framework within which we have to consider the structure of responsible life'.[39] For Bonhoeffer, this responsible life can be seen in the daily life that humans live: the father's responsibility to his children; the Statesperson's responsibility to the people she serves; the teacher's responsibility for and to his students. In each of these vocations, and in many others, we find a picture of the ethical, responsible human life.

But for Bonhoeffer, all of these are reflections of the one true human responsible agent, Jesus. He is the one who defines the responsible life for others through his vicarious representative action. Through his willingness to live for others, Jesus Christ reveals to humans what it means to be human, what it means to be responsible.

A remarkable feature of Bonhoeffer's ethical definition of Jesus through his vicarious representation is that Bonhoeffer had developed this notion in his very first work, *Sanctorum Communio*. In that work, Bonhoeffer laid out the lines of representation that would carry through to his *Ethics*. In *Sanctorum Communio*, the particularly Christian notion of representation is not that Christ simply acted for others, but that he did so in regard to bearing human sin and punishment. What Christ does is not a general activity of representation, but a particular work of representing humanity at the place where he, as the God-man, should never have had to go: the place of punishment. Christ enters into the place of sinful humanity as the one who would bear that sin vicariously for humanity. In bearing human sin, Christ does for humanity that which humanity could not do for itself: receive the grace of God and so be freed from the bonds of sin. In doing so, Christ not only is the vicarious representative for humanity, but he creates the new humanity that is free to be vicarious representative for others.

As has been mentioned, a remarkable feature of Bonhoeffer's conception of *Stellvertretung* in *Sanctorum Communio* is the way that it creates the foundation for Bonhoeffer's later action. Vicarious representation doesn't remain a theological idea for Bonhoeffer, but becomes a key reason for his willingness to act in the conspiracy against Hitler. In order to fight the tendency toward inaction due to a commitment to principles that was prevalent in the ethics of the church, Bonhoeffer finds in the Christological notion of vicarious representation a theological rationale for a willingness to act for the other even if that means entering into duplicitous actions by following the way of Christ into guilt and suffering. However, we are getting ahead of ourselves. We will explore the connection between vicarious representation and entering into suffering more fully in Chapter 5. For now, we must keep our eye on the way that Bonhoeffer understands vicarious representation and the ethical undergirding it gives to the responsible life.

As we return to *Ethics*, we do so for the sake of exploring the Christology of Bonhoeffer's understanding of responsibility. For Bonhoeffer, responsibility is the key to understanding the ethical action of Jesus Christ. Instead of seeing Christ as a moral exemplar, or as a man who came to provide new rules or principles, Bonhoeffer interprets Christ as the one who was willing to live a truly responsible life. It is important to keep in mind that Bonhoeffer understands human personhood as a personhood in community, by which he means that to be human is to be in relationship with others. Sin breaks this fundamental communion and creates atomistic individuals who seek to justify themselves through adherence to principles. However, Christ reveals what it means to be truly human: loving God and neighbor through responsible action on behalf of others, or, being for others. The human that is broken off from relationship with others through sin doesn't recognize the claim that the other places on me. But Jesus Christ reveals God's intent for humanity against the fallen humanity. True humanity is the humanity that recognizes the need for the other, and the responsibility that the other places on me. It is only in so living that humanity is as God intended. In Jesus' life, we see the responsible life of vicarious representation modeled. Bonhoeffer writes:

> Jesus – the life, our life – the Son of God who became human, lived as our vicarious representative. Through him, therefore, all human life is in its essence vicarious representation. Jesus was not the individual who sought to achieve some personal perfection, but only lived as the one who in himself has taken on and bears the selves of all human beings. His entire living, acting, and suffering was vicarious representative action. All that human beings were supposed to live, do, and suffer was fulfilled in him. In this real vicarious representative action, in which his human existence consists, he is the responsible human being par excellence.[40]

We find in this paragraph Bonhoeffer's central thoughts on vicarious representation, and so his central thoughts on Jesus Christ and his importance for understanding the ethical life. We see that Jesus became incarnate for the sake of living a vicarious representative life. Bonhoeffer will never speak of Jesus Christ in a transcendent eminence 'out there'. He can only be known and understood in his relationship to humans, and this relationship is a relationship of vicarious representation. To think of Jesus Christ apart from his work as our *Stellvertreter* is to seriously misunderstand Jesus Christ. This is consistent with what we have seen in the Christology lectures, where Bonhoeffer's emphasis is on the present Christ and his call to the human logos to obey. Bonhoeffer is uninterested in Christological conversations that remove Christ from history and seek to understand him through the relations of his two natures. Bonhoeffer is interested in the pattern of life that Jesus lived, and the revelation of true humanity that we see in his way of life.

The second thing that is summarized in this paragraph is how Jesus' vicarious representation becomes the defining factor of what it means to be human. Bonhoeffer argues here that because Christ lived a vicarious life for others, this is the only way to truly define what it is to be human. We will see in our investigation of the church in Chapter 3 how this plays itself out in Bonhoeffer' understanding of the church as the place where the new humanity of Christ is realized through her life for others.

The final point to be highlighted is the way that Bonhoeffer connects vicarious representative actions and the responsible human life. To be human is to be responsible for others. This is pivotal for understanding Bonhoeffer's actions in the conspiracy. While many other church leaders struggled with their response to Hitler, failing to act on behalf of the Jews and other victims of the Nazi regime, Bonhoeffer chose to act, and this action cannot be understood apart form his theology of representation. Because Christ lived his life for others in responsible action, so must the follower of Christ. For Christ, this responsibility meant the willingness to take on the guilt of human sin. Christ did not keep himself apart from the fallen world and from the sin of humans, but entered that world, taking upon himself the judgment of God that was ours. By going to the place of sin and judgment, by dying on the cross, Jesus expresses ultimately what it means to be human: being responsible for others. For Bonhoeffer, to be a true follower of Christ did not mean avoiding the guilt of sin by staying out of the conspiracy, but entering into it in order to be responsible for others. The call to responsible living is the call to suffering with Christ on behalf of others, a theme to which we will return in Chapter 5.

For now, we return to the prison letters. In this chapter, we have seen the way that Jesus Christ is at the center of Bonhoeffer's theology. We cannot understand the trajectory of Bonhoeffer's life, nor his ethical decisions, apart from his Christology. As Bonhoeffer's theology developed, his theology continued to revolve around the central question of the person of Christ and of his call to follow him. At the heart of this is Bonhoeffer's searching question: 'Who is Jesus Christ, for us, today?'

ONCE AGAIN: WHO IS JESUS CHRIST, FOR US, TODAY?

In this chapter, we have investigated the centrality of Bonhoeffer's Christology by looking at his understanding of Christ as the Man for Others who exists not simply in past history, but, just as importantly, in the present as well. Jesus Christ exists as and for humanity. He is not to be understood merely as an interesting historical figure, but as the present, life-giving Lord of all.

As we return again to the letter of 30 April, 1944, we can now better grasp the importance of the question that Bonhoeffer asks. The question is not: 'Who was Jesus when he lived two-thousand years ago?' but 'Who is Jesus *today*?' Who is Jesus here and now, at this point in history, and in this time and place? The answer to this question, for Bonhoeffer, is that the Jesus who is present today is the Jesus who is the Man for Others. Jesus, as the one who is the Counter-Logos and the vicarious representative of humanity, is the one who enters into the place of fallen humanity and acts on behalf of that humanity, going to the place where humanity was through her rejection of God, the place of suffering and death. Jesus is the one who bears the cross and enters into the place of rejection. He does this in order to open up humanity to reconciliation and newness of life with God. Bonhoeffer's question, 'who is Jesus Christ?', is answered: Jesus is the Man for Others. Jesus is the one whose existence is love for the other, and who demonstrates that love through suffering for humanity in order to restore her to new life.

As we have seen, Bonhoeffer's question about Jesus Christ is always also an ethical question. Jesus is the one who acts for others, and this creates for Bonhoeffer an ethical template of life for others. To be human, to follow in the way of Christ, is to be for others. As we turn our attention now to Bonhoeffer's ecclesiology, we will continue to see the importance of being for others and its impact on Bonhoeffer's understanding of the church.

CHAPTER 3

'THE CHURCH IS THE CHURCH ONLY WHEN IT EXISTS FOR OTHERS': BONHOEFFER'S ECCLESIOLOGY

In the previous chapter, we investigated the Christological center of Bonhoeffer's theology, and saw that we cannot approach the development of Bonhoeffer's thought apart from a recognition of this thoroughly Christocentric approach. In the prison letters, Bonhoeffer answered his question 'Who is Jesus Christ for us today' with his final Christological statement that Jesus is 'the Man for Others'. In turning now to Bonhoeffer's ecclesiology, it is our task to demonstrate the way in which the Church is the second key element of Bonhoeffer's theology. Bonhoeffer couples his description of Jesus as the Man for Others with a description of the church in its existence for others, as indicated by the phrase I have chosen as the title of this chapter: 'the church is the church only when it exists for others'.[1] From his earliest days, Bonhoeffer was concerned with explicating the reality of Christ that takes form in the reality of the concrete Christian community, the church. We have already seen how the theme 'Christ existing as community' functions as a model for understanding the relationship between the resurrected Christ and the church in history. As such, it is only when we have these two elements in place, Christ and the community, that we can see the grounding of Bonhoeffer's thought that will carry him through to his final days, and to the thoughts that are formed in his letters from prison.

THE CHURCH FOR OTHERS

Before we take our journey through Bonhoeffer's ecclesiology, let's first take a closer look at the phrase that is the theme of this chapter, 'the church for others'. As has been indicated, Bonhoeffer's final and most robust definition of Christ is 'the Man for Others'. In the last chapter, we saw that this is the answer to Bonhoeffer's question, 'Who is Christ, for us, today?' Christ is the one who is there for us, who exists as the meaning and center of history and existence, and whose very self is identified by his 'being for others'. Christ overcomes the sin of the world through his self-giving, reversing the effects of the *cor curvum in se* and thereby setting humanity free to once again love one another and live in the communion that God intended. Jesus is the new humanity, in whom the reality of redeemed human life has dawned, and in whom love of God and neighbor was truly demonstrated and thus created in history.

Given this description of Jesus, it becomes clear that the church can only be described in the same terms. The phrase 'the church is the church only when it exists for others' is found, not in a letter, but in the outline for a book that Bonhoeffer composed during his time in prison. Bonhoeffer is turning his thoughts to the book he will write after the war, and at the heart of this is the place of the church in post-war Germany. Bonhoeffer was disillusioned by the self-protection and defensive posture of the Confessing Church in the 1930s, a position that led ultimately to splintering and an ineffective witness for Christ against the Nazis. Instead of becoming a unified movement based around a clear sense of the Lordship of Christ that stands opposed to any human claims of being 'Führer' and opposed to the work of the State in its attacks on human life, the church instead made its goal *self-preservation*. This clarified for Bonhoeffer the fundamental error that caused the church to fail in its resistance to Hitler: the church operated for herself and not for others. Her desire to keep a slice of power and respectability meant that she sacrificed her true calling of being for those who were victims of the Third Reich. The church failed because she misunderstood the ethical nature of the call of Christ to be for others, no matter who those others are, even Jews.

In his reflections on this failure of the Confessing Church and his thinking about the church of the future, it is clear that Bonhoeffer was pondering radical changes in the structure and form of the church. He suggests that the church should give away all its property, and that the clergy should live off of good will offerings, or get a paying job that would support his church ministry. Both of these are statements that reveal the depth of the questions, and possible solutions, that Bonhoeffer was pondering as he was rethinking the future of the church in Germany. In another place, Bonhoeffer suggests that the church will have only two tasks after the war: 'prayer and righteous action'.[2] Bonhoeffer believed that, because of her failure to speak out against the Nazis, the church had lost her voice in society, and thus she must remain silent for a time. He says that there will be a time to speak again, but until that time, the church must pray and do. The church must act, not for herself, but for those whom Christ came to save: the poor, the oppressed, the outcasts. To be a follower of Jesus Christ, the Man for Others, is to be included in a community of disciples who, like their Lord, exist for others. This is Bonhoeffer's theological vision of the church.

With this brief introduction to Bonhoeffer's conception of the church from his time in prison, we are now in a position to look back in his theology and more closely identify the ecclesial thread that runs through his work. We will begin, as we did in the last chapter, with Bonhoeffer's early theology from *Sanctorum Communio* and *Act and Being*, and once again interact with the theme 'Christ existing as community'. In the last chapter we stressed the Christological implications of that phrase, or '*Christ* existing as community', while here we will stress the ecclesiological implications, or 'Christ existing as *community*'.

In moving now to our formal discussion of Bonhoeffer's ecclesiology, we do so with the Christological foundation firmly in place. As I have argued, Bonhoeffer's ecclesiology can only be grasped from the perspective of his Christology, for from beginning to end, Bonhoeffer consistently sees the Church as the community in whom Christ is being formed (Gal. 4:13). Bonhoeffer asserts the uniqueness of the social form of the church precisely because of her relation to Christ. In fact, it is this very notion of the formation of Christ in the church-community that makes the church the church, that makes it understandable only from the perspective of revelation, and that makes it in fact to *be* revelation.

THE CHURCH IN *SANCTORUM COMMUNIO* AND *ACT AND BEING*

The church is the place where Christ dwells through the Spirit; the church *is* 'Christ existing as community'. Bonhoeffer is committed to the church from his earliest days, a concern that arises from a firm commitment to the revealed truth that the church is the place where Christ is present on the earth. As such, the church should and must take on the character of Christ; or, perhaps a better way to say it, the church must recognize that it is the community on earth in which the form of Christ is being formed. Because of the import of this notion for Bonhoeffer, we must attend to his understanding not merely that Christ is present, but *how* the form of Christ takes form in the church. In other words, our investigation of the church in *Sanctorum Communio* will center us on the transformation of the community of saints to the likeness of Christ, the Man for Others.

As we have seen, Bonhoeffer views the church as the Body of Christ, the place where Christ is present. But, of course, he is not so naïve as to assert that the church will be the perfected body of Christ on earth. Instead, Bonhoeffer recognizes that the church is and always will be marked by the imperfection of life in a fallen world. She is and will be, until the triumph of the ultimate, both the *corpus Christi* and the *corpus Adae*, the Body of Christ and the Body of Adam, or, the *peccatorum communio* (the community of sinners) and the *sanctorum communio* (the community of saints). The church is not the community of the perfected, but the community of the forgiven, the community of the justified, whose righteousness is hers in Christ, but whose righteousness is also hidden. What we see in Bonhoeffer's early ecclesiology is a communal example of Luther's theology of the *simul iustus et peccator*. As the individual human is both justified and sinner all at once, so the church community is a community of justified sinners.

Given this emphasis that the church is both justified and sinful, both the *sanctorum communio* and the *peccatorum communio*, one must ask the question of the transformation of the church.[3] If fallen humanity, humanity in Adam, is the *cor curvum in se*, how is this community transformed from being turned in on the self to being the community that exists for others? If Christ is present, in what way does the church *change*? If the church is 'Christ existing as community', in what way does she take on the character of her Lord? Isn't this demanded by the theology of otherness? In what way does the *peccatorum communio* become the *sanctorum communio*? Bonhoeffer's theology of 'being-for-others' is built on this conception of transformation, or, of formation of the nature of Christ in the church community. In what way is this expressed in *Sanctorum Communio*?

We need to be reminded at this point about Bonhoeffer's theology of sin, in which he understands that humanity has rejected her created intention by God. We have surrendered ourselves to the impulses of selfish desire, no longer being the creatures who love God and neighbor, but who love self.[4] As such, we live introverted lives, lives of broken communion with God and neighbor. This view of sinful humanity doesn't simply create individual sinners; instead, Bonhoeffer asserts that the fall creates a community of persons who are the collective person of humanity in sin, which he names the *peccatorum communio*. Her 'social basic-relations' are based on this atomistic self-orientation that marks humanity due to her rejection of God and of self in sin. But, as we have also seen, with Christ, there is a different social-basic relationality: Christ exists not for self, but for the other. Therefore, the uniqueness of the church as a social community is that her social-basic relation reflects the other-centeredness of Christ. We can put this more pointedly by saying that the church is unique because her *essence* is Jesus, the one who has rejected humanity's rejection of God, who has himself taken on the judgment of humanity in Adam and has thus created a new social basic-relation. Instead of Adam's atomistic self-seeking as the social basic-relation, Christ is now the new humanity, the one through whom humanity is created anew. Christ lived the life of ecstatic otherness, loving God and neighbor and rejecting the selfishness that marks the *peccatorum communio*. Christ is the 'Man for Others' because the social basic relation of his life was *love*, the divine love that we see at the cross and which can be defined only through the life and death of Jesus Christ. In Christ humanity is now free to live for others. In Christ there is no seeking after self in ways that are destructive to the other. In Christ there is love. And so the community of Christ, the community that *is* 'Christ existing as community' must become this humanity. But how does this occur?

The previous paragraph noted the idea that Christ has realized the new humanity. This notion is directly related to our earlier discussion of Christ as the *Stellvertreter*, the 'vicarious representative' who acts on behalf of fallen humanity by taking her sins into himself. He truly takes on Adam's sin and Adam is killed in Christ. But Christ is not killed; he arises as the new humanity. The realization of the new humanity in Christ is the first movement in the divine work of re-creating humanity. Now, the new humanity is created by God through the resurrection of Jesus Christ, and Jesus is himself this new humanity, and is the vicarious representative of all humanity. But the realized Christ is the resurrected eternal Christ who dwells in heaven with his Father. But how does the realized Christ become actualized on earth? Bonhoeffer asserts that, because of God's love for and commitment to creation and history, there can be no notion of the reality of Christ remaining in the heavenlies, separated from true human history. Instead, 'The church is God's new will and purpose for humanity. God's will is always directed toward the concrete, historical human being. But this means that it must be implemented *in history*'.[5] This implementation in history is the complement to the realization in eternity. As such, we see in Bonhoeffer's vision of the church the actualization of the new humanity through the work of the Spirit, as the new humanity that is realized in Christ becomes real in history. It is in this actualization that we come to see Christ taking form in history. But the actualization by the Spirit does not take Bonhoeffer's focus off of Christ. He writes, '. . . the significance of Christ must be made the focal point in the temporal actualization of the church'.[6]

The actualization of the church takes place as the Holy Spirit brings the Word of God to the community. Actualization 'is accomplished by the Spirit-impelled word of the crucified and risen Lord of the church. The Spirit can work only through this Word. . . . Tying the Spirit to the Word means that the Spirit aims at a plurality of hearers and establishes a visible sign by which the actualization is to take place'.[7] It is the Holy Spirit, then, who is the primary actor in bringing the new life of Christ, the life that turns away from the self and lives for others, into the community of the church. This work truly renews and transforms individuals who are members of the *peccatorum communio* and places them into the new community of Christ, the *sanctorum communio.* Here, in this renewed humanity, we have a foretaste of the life to come, and a renewal of the life that God intended for his human creatures.

We are now in a position to summarize our discussion of 'Christ existing as community' in *Sanctorum Communio* and its importance for our understanding of Bonhoeffer's ecclesiology. For Bonhoeffer, the church is a unique community because it has a unique nature: it *is* the Body of Christ, the presence of Christ on earth in history. This presence is the formation of a new being for the church, and thus a new social basic-relation. Humanity in Adam is the collective person of humanity whose social basic relation is atomistic and self-seeking;

humanity in Christ, the community of the church, reverses this social basic-relation, and instead is a community marked by the mutuality of Christian love in Christ. Thus, 'Christ existing as community' is of such important for grasping Bonhoeffer's ecclesiology because it is built on the Christological foundation and stresses the importance of viewing Christ and the community in close conjunction. Christ himself is the nature of the church; she is the community in whom Christ is being formed as the old humanity, the *peccatorum communio,* is superseded by the new humanity, the *sanctorum communio*. This doesn't mean that the church will achieve the perfection of God's life in this time, but it does mean that she is a community through whom the new life of Christ is expressed to all, both those within the community and those outside the community. Just as we see the foundation of Bonhoeffer's ethical actions for others in his Christology, so we see his insistence on the church's active life in participating in the sufferings of the world through a love for others rooted firmly in his understanding of the nature of the church that follows her Lord in existing for others.

THE CHURCH IN *LIFE TOGETHER*

Perhaps Bonhoeffer's most famous treatise on community is his short work *Life Together*. This text was written during Bonhoeffer's time leading the Confessing Church seminary at Finkenwalde, which became for him something of a lab for his reflections on the communal life of the church. During this time, Bonhoeffer literally lived life together with his students, as they all occupied a large home, in which they slept, ate, studied, and learned. Bonhoeffer also took his seminarians on numerous journeys, traveling around the area on bicycles to minister in local Confessing Churches, or going for a trip to the sea to relax from the rigors of study in an illegal seminary. Throughout all of this, Bonhoeffer was thinking more deeply about the concrete reality of a community of disciples who would live out the life of Christ for others. In the previous section, we reviewed Bonhoeffer's understanding of the communal import of Bonhoeffer's notion 'Christ existing as community', seeing the theological foundation of Bonhoeffer's ecclesiology. In *Life Together* we find, not a theoretical discussion of the nature of the church, but a concrete reflection on the life of a community of disciples seeking to live out his life together.

The presence of Christ in the community of disciples is visible from the outset of the book, as Bonhoeffer makes the connection between Christ and the church through a parallel to the sacraments. In the community, the invisible Christ is present in and through each member, and so he is recognized in the fellowship of the church. The members of the community 'receive and meet one another as one meets the Lord, in reverence, humility and joy. They receive each other's blessings as the blessing of the Lord Jesus Christ'.[8] Because the church is the Body of Christ, the place where he is present through the work of the Holy Spirit, the community is the presence of Christ to one another. As such, the church is 'a gracious anticipation of the end time',[9] and her life together around the Word and sacrament is a gift of God's grace.[10] In this gracious anticipation of the future, the church is called to hear the Word of God, which is the means through which the Spirit works to build up the church. Bonhoeffer's focus in *Life Together* on the Word and the sacraments indicate that the work of the Spirit is tied to concrete means, through which God is at work to build up a concrete community. Bonhoeffer does not conceive of the church as a spiritual community, but a physical body that cannot be comprehended through the lens of duality. Christ became a concrete human being, and so the church must be understood, not as a spiritual community, but as a concrete historical community that is given life through the nourishment of the Word, but also through the physical means of the bread and wine. We will more closely examine his emphasis on the physical when we turn our attention to worldliness in the next chapter.

Moving forward, the centrality of Christ to the Christian community is made clearer yet: 'Christian community means community through Jesus Christ and in Jesus Christ. There is no Christian community that is more than this, and none that is less than this. . . . We belong to one another only through and in Jesus Christ'. Bonhoeffer emphasizes the centrality of Christ through a discussion of his mediatorial role in the community. His assertion is that there are no unmediated relationships in the community of faith. Because Christ is present and is central to the community, and because it is Christ's new humanity that is being formed in the Body of Christ, it follows that he stands between all relationships of his followers. Relationships that don't recognize the mediating presence of Christ become relationships of power in which the other is used for the sake of the self; these relationships typify the *cor curvum in se*, in which persons don't

Crooked heart

exist for the sake of the other, but the other exists for the sake of the self. Concerning Christ's mediating role, Bonhoeffer writes:

> Without Jesus Christ there is discord between God and humanity and between one human being and another. Christ has become the mediator who has made peace with God and peace among human beings. . . . Christ opened up the way to God and to one another. Now Christians can live with each other in peace; they can love and serve one another; they can become one. But they can continue to do so only through Jesus Christ. Only in Jesus Christ are we one; only through him are we bound together.[11]

When the community doesn't recognize the centrality of Christ, there is the danger of becoming a false community. Bonhoeffer distinguishes between two kinds of community: the spiritual, which is based on the presence of Christ through the Word of God and the Holy Spirit, and the psychic, which is based on human will and emotion. The psychic community is based on 'a wishful image' created by human desires for community on their own terms. Instead of allowing God to create the community as he desires, humans seek their own based on their own desire for community instead of for the sake of Christ. Psychic community may be well-intentioned, but because it is not based on the centrality of Christ and his mediatorial presence, it inevitably fails. Distinguishing between these two kinds of community, Bonhoeffer asserts that 'the foundation of Christian community is truth; the basis of emotional community is desire'.[12] The problem with desire is that, if it is not based on Christ's love, it can easily become a desire that seeks the self and not the other. Remembering that the new humanity in Christ is the humanity that is for others, while the old humanity of Adam seeks the self, we can see how a desire for community that arises out of human desire and not the love of Christ is a community of the *cor curvum in se*. As such, there is a desire for communion with other souls that feeds the desire of self-centered people, but isn't the communion of those who exist for others. We read, '[I]n the self-centered community there exists a profound, elemental emotional desire for community. . . . Here is where self-centered, strong persons enjoy life to the full, securing for themselves the admiration, the love, or the fear of the weak.'[13]

In contrast to this, spiritual love centered on Christ 'loves the other for the sake of Christ'.[14] There is no desire for self that intermingles with love for the other; instead, because Christ is central and is the one who is desired, the self is free to truly love and give the self to the other. Because Christ is recognized as the mediator, there is no need for unmediated access to the other. The self doesn't need the other for her own sake, but can love the other for the sake of Christ. In fact, Christ himself directs that love and 'will tell me what love for my brothers and sisters really looks like'.[15] The self doesn't know what true love is but must learn from Christ how to love. Here we see clearly the connection between Christ and the community, and the fact that, for Bonhoeffer, there is no community without Christ, but also no Christ without community.

The first half of this chapter has established the clarity with which Bonhoeffer views the relation between Christ and the church. Christ is the being of the church whose new humanity enlivens and transforms the church community. Through this transformation, the church is conformed to Christ, who exists for others, and so itself takes on his being for others in her existence. But as we move forward, it is time to turn our attention toward the church's relation to the world. We do so by bringing our findings from this point and move forward to set up our discussion in Chapter 4 on our final foundation theme: worldliness. What is the relationship between the church and the world? We will investigate this question by working through *Discipleship* and *Ethics*.

THE CHURCH IN *DISCIPLESHIP*

In our discussion of *Discipleship* in Chapter 2, we highlighted Bonhoeffer's emphasis on the cross in that work, noting the historical context and evaluating the way that the context encouraged Bonhoeffer's focus on discipleship as following after the suffering Christ. As we turn now to the church in *Discipleship*, we see that Bonhoeffer doesn't envision discipleship as a solitary activity of an individual, but instead we see an emphasis on the community who together walk the way of the suffering Christ, acknowledging him as Lord and going the way that he directs.

One of the key ways that Bonhoeffer describes this community who lives under the Lordship of Christ is 'the community of the cross'. To explore Bonhoeffer's notion of the community of the cross, we will focus our attention in this section on baptism in *Discipleship*. As noted earlier, Bonhoeffer notes that the notion of discipleship falls out of usage in the later New Testament, particularly in the Pauline epistles. Instead, we read of baptism. Where for the contemporaries of Jesus the call of Christ functioned as the means of calling people from their former lives to following after him, for those who would be called later in history the means of the call is baptism. Baptism, then, is the means by which the Christ who is present today calls through Scripture for an obedient response to His Lordship. This call is an offer from God, not something we offer to God. Instead of seeing baptism as primarily our act of service to God, we must understand it has his gracious call on our lives by which we are called out of our lives of rejecting God and into reconciled fellowship with him.

Baptism, of course, is not an individualistic conception, but is the means by which God creates the church. Bonhoeffer writes, 'Baptism thus implies a break. Christ invades the realm of Satan and lays hold of those who belong to him, thus creating his church community.'[16] The creation of the church community through baptism parallels the creation of the discipleship community by the original call of Christ to his followers. When he called Peter, John, Andrew, and the others, he called them into a fellowship, into a community. When he calls women and men through the Word to be baptized, Jesus calls them not merely away *from* their old lives, but more importantly *to* a new life in community with Jesus and those who together follow him along the way. But this break with the old is more than a removal – it is a death. In baptism, the individual is called away from her old life by being put to death with Christ. But this death is not a vindictive act of an angry God; instead, it is the gracious call of God to restore his followers to life and to remove them from the destructive presence of sin. The act of baptism is inseparable from the community of the cross. In baptism, the community of the cross is formed, and through baptism the church participates in the cross of Jesus Christ.

Baptism is the one death that the Christian must die. Baptism is not something that needs to be repeated, as it is into the one death of Christ that the Christian is baptized. There is in Scripture an emphasis on daily dying with Christ; Bonhoeffer interprets this, however, not as a repetition of the once and for all death that takes place at baptism but as a daily remembrance of Christ's one death and of the disciple's participation in that death at baptism. The Eucharist is the sacrament by which the death at baptism is continually recollected.

When the disciple partakes of the bread and wine, she is recollecting the one death of Christ in which she has been baptized once and for all. Baptism is the one entry into community with Christ's body; the Eucharist is the continual remembrance of our entry into this community. Bonhoeffer states, 'Baptism incorporates us as members into the unity of the Body of Christ. The Lord's supper keeps us in this community with Christ's body.'[17] The church is created through the sacrament of baptism and continues to live from that baptism. The death of Christ is the beginning of new life, and the church is that community who lives this new life through the gracious death at baptism.

Baptism creates the Body of Christ, the place of communion with Jesus. The church is unique because it lives in continual intimate communion with Christ. In thinking of the Body of Christ, Bonhoeffer asserts this quite literally: fellowship with Jesus is bodily fellowship in which the bodily human is accepted by God. We will spend more time on the nature of Bonhoeffer's theology of creation and the importance of the bodily in the next chapter. But in anticipation of this, let us note here that Bonhoeffer never views the church that is created through death and baptism in 'spiritual' terms alone. When Bonhoeffer thinks of the church, he thinks of a concrete community of human beings who are present in history in bodily form, and present in history as the Body of Christ. Jesus came to earth in the flesh, was killed bodily, and was raised to new life in human flesh. To think of the church, then, as a spiritual entity is to mistake the nature of God's mission in Christ. Christ came to claim humanity for God. To do this is to create a new Body of flesh and blood which is the place of Jesus Christ. The Word of God has truly become flesh, and the Word of God truly redeems humans in the flesh, not taking them out of their bodies, but restoring them to bodily life. One of the key points in Bonhoeffer's ecclesiology is that the church is to be a community of the cross who has its sin borne in the flesh of Jesus Christ in order that they might live concrete, fleshly lives as new humans.

The last point to be made here is the connection between *Discipleship* and *Sanctorum Communio*. In our analysis of *Sanctorum Communio*, we discussed Bonhoeffer's notion of the actualization of the new humanity in history through the work of the Holy Spirit. This theme once again comes to the fore in *Discipleship*, demonstrating the coherence between Bonhoeffer's early ecclesiology and his view of the church in the mid-1930s. Although he doesn't use the terminology of realization/actualization, the emphasis on the work of the Spirit as the means through which the new life of Christ is present is clear. In his discussion of baptism, the role of the Spirit is critical: Christ is present through the Spirit, who leads the disciple into deeper intimacy with Christ. This emphasis advances the pneumatology of *Sanctorum Communio*. Bonhoeffer's strong emphasis in *Discipleship* on the presence of Christ is pneumatological in its shape. The Spirit mediates Christ's presence, and so it is the Spirit who creates the church community at baptism. The community of the cross is a community of the Spirit. The emphasis on the presence of Christ through the actualizing work of the Spirit is most clearly evident in the following claim: 'Through the Holy Spirit, the crucified and risen Christ exists as the church-community, as the "new human being".'[18]

Before we move on, we must make some comments regarding Bonhoeffer's discussion of separation from the world in *Discipleship.* For some interpreters of Bonhoeffer, his emphasis on the distinction between the church and the world in this work is contradictory to the later emphasis in Bonhoeffer on the importance of the world and the church being a community that exists for the world. The Bonhoeffer of the prison letters, even the Bonhoeffer of *Ethics*, would not make such statements of separation as the Bonhoeffer of *Discipleship* does. Undoubtedly, there are statements that Bonhoeffer makes in this text that sound foreign to his later thinking. The historical situation in the mid-1930s created a strong emphasis for Bonhoeffer on the need for the church to stand apart and to follow the way of Christ. There is, no doubt, in his tone a sense of the dangers of the world that he will later drop. We must note the differences between *Discipleship* and Bonhoeffer's later theology, but we also must not make too much of this distinction.

As for the differences, I have already made mention of the historical setting as influential on Bonhoeffer's presentation of the relation between the church and the world in *Discipleship*. Because of his desire to call the church to follow the costly way of Christ and because of the dangers he sees in the church's accommodation to the powers of the world, Bonhoeffer's clear focus in discipleship is to call Christ's followers to die to self and go the way of suffering. This emphasis on death and suffering will not fade in Bonhoeffer's later theology, though there will be a stronger emphasis on life that brings balance to his theology of death. But what will fade is the language of separation. To understand why this is so, we need to recognize that it is not only the historical situation that is influencing Bonhoeffer's thinking here, but there is also a theological influence. In *Discipleship*, Bonhoeffer is operating with a view that he later calls (and rejects) 'thinking in two spheres'.[19] In *Discipleship*, Bonhoeffer's understanding of Christ's Lordship is limited to the church: the church is the community over which Christ is Lord. Because of this, Bonhoeffer speaks strongly of the separation between the church and the world, which leads him to assert that the church must carve out space for itself on earth. He writes, 'The Body of Christ takes up physical space here on earth.'[20] Later, we read, 'The "ekklesia" of Christ, the community of disciples, is no longer subject to the rule of this world. True, it lives in the midst of the world. But it already has been made into one body. It is a territory with an authority of its own, a space set apart.'[21] In these statements, Bonhoeffer's emphasis on the separateness of the church in *Discipleship* is clear, and this is a theological emphasis that Bonhoeffer will later view as incomplete. By thinking in two spheres, Bonhoeffer underestimates the place of Christ in the world, and thus runs the danger of creating an ecclesiology in which the church carves out its own space on earth instead of his later emphasis, in which the church's role is to proclaim the Lordship of Christ over all the earth, an emphasis we saw in our investigation of Bonhoeffer's Christology in the last chapter.

Though we see some clear evolution of Bonhoeffer's theology in his later thinking, I suggest that Bonhoeffer's emphasis on separation in *Discipleship* is a necessary, though not final, statement about the church that gives us a complete view of Bonhoeffer's understanding of the relation of the church to the world. Yes, the historical situation perhaps caused him to overstate his statements about the church's separation from the world in *Discipleship*, but we must realize that there is a certain emphasis on separation even in the prison letters themselves. In the letter of 21 July 1944 Bonhoeffer refers to the kind of relation between the follower of Christ he *is* talking about, and makes it clear what he is *not* talking about. He writes, 'During the last year I've come to know and understand more and more the profound this worldliness of Christianity. . . . I don't mean the shallow and banal this worldliness of the enlightened, the busy, the comfortable, or the lascivious, but the profound this worldliness, characterized by discipline and the constant knowledge of death and resurrection.'[22] There is a way for the church to live rightly in the world, and a way to live wrongly in the world. To live rightly in the world is to do so with the discipline of Christ and a constant remembrance of his death and resurrection, and so a constant participation in that death and resurrection. The key point here is this: through death, the church is separated from the world, and through life the church is sent back into the world as a unique community. We read, 'The difference between the Christian hope of resurrection and the mythological hope is that the former sends a man back to his life on earth in a wholly new way which is even more sharply defined that it is in the Old Testament.'[23] Bonhoeffer's emphasis on separation in *Discipleship* is incomplete, and reflects a failure in Bonhoeffer's theology at this stage to identify the fullness of Christ's Lordship over the whole world. However, the church is related to the world as the community in whom Christ is dying, so separating the church from the 'lascivious' worldliness, but is also the community in whom the new life of Christ is taking form, so sending the church back into the world in a whole new way. This discussion shows us that Bonhoeffer's emphasis on the church in *Discipleship*, though incomplete, cannot be disregarded out of hand. The separation seen in this work is part and parcel of Bonhoeffer's later theology. If we fail to regard Bonhoeffer's theology in *Discipleship*, we will fail to grasp the kind of relation between the church and the world that Bonhoeffer later describes in the prison letters.

THE CHURCH IN THE PRISON LETTERS

We have seen throughout this chapter the way that Bonhoeffer's Christology has determined and shaped his ecclesiology. In many ways, we can say that Bonhoeffer's ecclesiology is simply his Christology placed into the context of community. In Chapter 2 we analyzed how Bonhoeffer emphasizes the presence of Christ as determinative for his understanding of Jesus and his relation to the world. In the Christology lectures in particular we observed this emphasis: there, Bonhoeffer begins with an emphasis on the present Christ, and only after this turns to investigate the Christ of history. His overriding question in the prison letters is 'who is Jesus Christ, for us, today?'; he does not do away with the historical Jesus, or place a wedge between the Jesus of history and the Christ of faith, a hallmark of liberal theology, but rather maintains an emphasis on the unity between the historical Christ and the present Christ. However, his dominant question regards the present Christ: who is he? What difference does he make? How can he be proclaimed as Lord in a world come of age? As Bonhoeffer walks through the relation between Christ and the church, his emphasis on the present Christ remains in his formulation 'Christ existing as community'. When one investigates the community of the church, one is looking at the community in which Christ is present. Christ is the ontological center of the church, and so Christ and the church must be thought of together.

We see this unity in the theme that is our theme in this chapter: 'The church is the church only when she exists for others.' This, of course, is an echo of Bonhoeffer's definitive notion of Christ: 'the Man for Others'. The new humanity, realized in Christ and actualized in history in the community of the church, is to be for others. This definition is the reversal of the fall, in which humans turn from the other and exist as the *cor curvum in se*.

There is another theme in the prison letters that helps us to examine the ecclesiology of Bonhoeffer's final theological period. We raised the question earlier in this chapter regarding the relationship between the church and the world. Some have suggested that Bonhoeffer has dropped his emphasis on the church by the prison letters, and instead of seeing a unique community of the church, there is rather an abandoning of the church in the prison letters, as it is deemed unnecessary by his emphasis on the Lordship of Christ over the whole world. In *Discipleship*, we see a strong emphasis on the church, which some argue is a result of the 'thinking in two spheres' phase of Bonhoeffer's development. He later rejects the two spheres; does he therefore need the church? If Christ is Lord of the whole world, what use is there for a church?

I believe that this is an inaccurate understanding of Bonhoeffer, and suggest that the church remains a key fixture of Bonhoeffer's later theology. Although he has rejected the thinking in two spheres, this does not eliminate for Bonhoeffer an important place for the church. We can see this clearly through an interaction with another theme in the prison letters, the *disciplina arcani*, or 'the discipline of the secret'.[24] Bonhoeffer makes reference to the secret discipline in two places in the prison letters. While these references are brief and somewhat difficult to decipher, Andreas Pangritz has demonstrated that they are deeply rooted in Bonhoeffer's theology, and as such should not be seen as inconsequential based on the relative lack of references.[25] John Matthews argues that we cannot dismiss the importance of this theme due simply to the relatively few overt mentions of it in Bonhoeffer's writings. He writes, 'Although Bonhoeffer's extant writings reveal only three specific references to it, the concept of *disciplina arcani* was central to Bonhoeffer's entire theological orientation.'[26] So while the number of reference may be few, the importance of the theme in not inconsequential.

What does Bonhoeffer mean by the *disciplina arcani*, and what does it tell us about his ecclesiology in the final phase of his life? Bonhoeffer adopts this term from the practice of the early church in which the church prepared people for baptism. In the first centuries of the church's existence, those who presented themselves to the church desiring to become members of the community were put through a three-year catechesis, by which they were trained in the mysteries of the Christian faith. Only at the end of this time were they allowed to be baptized and join the community. The purpose of this training was, in Bonhoeffer's understanding, to 'protect the mysteries of the faith from profanation', an emphasis in his rejection of Barth's positivism of revelation. In Bonhoeffer's critique of Barth's theological project he suggests that Barth, instead of following through with his initial project of critiquing religion, instead ends up establishing a doctrinal system in which each level of theological reasoning is as important as any other. As such, Bonhoeffer believes that the positivism of revelation fails to recognize the importance of the mysteries of the faith, and fails to recognize that not all doctrine should be taken on the same level. Instead of Barth's 'like it or lump it' approach, Bonhoeffer suggests a restoration of the discipline of the secret, by which the mysteries of the faith are protected.

Matthews argues that this notion is best defined as 'a responsible sharing of the mystery of Christian faith'.[27] What Bonhoeffer proposes here is a recognition that the Christian faith is prone to profanation if her teachings are not handled with care. The early church did not want for anyone to be told the depths of the teaching of the church. Instead, the early church protected the mysteries of the faith through the discipline of the secret, through a responsible sharing of the mysteries of the faith by which it resisted casting the pearls of the gospel before swine. Instead of an irresponsible speaking of the mysteries of Christianity, the early church recognized the wisdom of protecting the faith from profanation. Bonhoeffer argues that Barth's doctrinal approach, in which every teaching of doctrine has equal weight, fails to incorporate this wisdom. Barth ends up with a view of doctrine in which there are no true mysteries, but a system by which doctrine can be fully disclosed.

What does this say for the church? Matthews argues that the *disciplina arcani* must not be used to re-establish the thinking in two spheres that Bonhoeffer rejects.[28] In other words, the notion of the discipline of the secret cannot be seen as a desire for Bonhoeffer to establish 'a more private, personal, inward, spiritual practice of faith to complement the more public, communal, outward deeds of justice'. Instead, he proposes, the *disciplina arcani* is reflective of 'Bonhoeffer's intent . . . to reinstate a careful discipline in every realm of life, private and public, personal and communal, inward and outward, spiritual and physical.'[29] While I agree with Matthews that we cannot use the discipline of the secret to re-establish two spheres thinking, we can see in this a statement about the place of the church in a world come of age. Matthews rightly indicates that the discipline of the secret cannot be understood *only* to be statement of the private, but it can be seen partially as that. Bonhoeffer nowhere indicates that the church becomes obsolete in the world come of age. Instead, we see Bonhoeffer doing some significant rethinking of the place and role of the church, but not a replacement of the church. As such, the discipline of the secret becomes an insight into Bonhoeffer's later ecclesiology. He envisages a church that meets in private, and that recognizes the importance of protecting the mysteries of the faith. He foresees a church that disciples people and in whom the form of Christ is formed as a testimony to the world of the new humanity in Christ. He desires a church that doesn't live in two spheres, but wholeheartedly in the midst of the world. However, though this doesn't eliminate the 'inner' nature of the church, it does shape Bonhoeffer's understanding of the inner nature of the church. The discipline of the secret is critical to the formation of Christ through responsible discipleship that gives the church its mission in the world: being for others.

This brings us back to the theme of our chapter: 'the church is the church only when it exists for others'. Through the formation of the new humanity in Christ, the church is redeemed from the fallen emphasis on self that marks the old humanity to become the new humanity of Christ that exists for others. From *Sanctorum Communio* through to the prison correspondence, we have seen the importance of the church in Bonhoeffer's theology, and have seen the centrality of Christ to his ecclesiology. Both are marked by existence for others.

Critical to Bonhoeffer's understanding of the church is his experience with the Confessing Church in the 1930s. Though the groundwork of his ecclesiology was laid in the late 1920s, it is truly his experience with the Confessing Church that clarifies his vision. His involvement with this movement led him to see the failure of a church that fights for its own status and power instead of for those who have no status or power. His involvement with the ecumenical movement during this same period demonstrated for him how easily the church can become tribal, failing to maintain her allegiance to Christ rather than to country. Bonhoeffer's disappointment with the church in the 1930s opens up the way to an ecclesiology that moves beyond a church of self-interest to a church for others. Bonhoeffer sees in Jesus Christ a Man whose being is defined as for others, and so the church is the community in whom Christ is formed, the church that is the place where 'Christ exists as community', must reflect her Lord in its being for others. A church that exists for herself and not for others is not the true church over which Christ is Lord.

To this point in our exploration of Bonhoeffer's theology we have explored our first two foundational themes: Christ and the church. The relation between the two has been made evident. In the next chapter, we turn to our third foundational theme: worldliness. As we will see, a survey of Bonhoeffer's conception of worldliness follows on naturally from Christ and the church. If, as we have seen, Bonhoeffer defines both Christ and the church as being for others, the question arises: being for whom? For Bonhoeffer, the answer to this question is clear: for the creation that God created and called good. God values very highly the creation, demonstrating this through the incarnation of Christ and his work to redeem the creation. It is to this emphasis on worldliness that we now turn.

CHAPTER 4

THE WORLD COME OF AGE: WORLDLINESS IN BONHOEFFER

Having now engaged two central themes in Bonhoeffer's theology, we turn to the third critical theme that we are using as a guide for understanding Bonhoeffer: worldliness. Up to this point, we have made passing references to the importance of the concrete world for Bonhoeffer. We have seen this in his emphasis on the incarnation of Christ, and how this led to his early critique that Barth's actualism didn't do justice to the entry of God into the world as a concrete human being. Because of this, Barth doesn't simply fail to grasp the nature of Christ, but also the importance of the world. Similarly, we have seen Bonhoeffer's continued expression of the church as a thoroughly historical and concrete community. Never in Bonhoeffer's theology is the church to live an existence removed from the world. As we have seen over the past two chapters, his insistence on Christ as truly incarnate and entering into history creates for him a focus on Christ's action in history for others. Christ truly took on human flesh and entered into the world with all its suffering and failure. Following from this, the church is called to truly be in the world as the concrete presence of Christ for others. Our emphasis to this point on Christ and on the church leads us naturally to an investigation of the world in Bonhoeffer's theology.

'THE WORLD COME OF AGE': AN INITIAL INVESTIGATION

In his letter of 8 June 1944, Bonhoeffer describes the process of the world's maturation to the point of becoming 'the world come of age'.[1] For Bonhoeffer, this involves humanity becoming autonomous, coming to that stage in human history where humanity 'has learnt to deal with himself in all questions of importance without recourse to the "working hypothesis" called "God".'[2] For Bonhoeffer, this development, which he believes began in the thirteenth century, has been brought to a completion. Prior to this development in human history, the big questions, the questions of how the cosmos works, of how humanity was created, of who is in control of the seasons and the weather, were all answered by 'God'. But now, humanity no longer needs the answer 'God'. The question of how the universe functions, how humanity came to be, and how the weather works have all been answered by human reason through scientific discovery. As such, 'God' is no longer a needed hypothesis. Humanity has become autonomous, and human reason replaces God as the undoubted object of faith. We read, '[I]t is becoming evident that everything gets along without "God" – and, in fact, just as well as before. As in the scientific field, so in human affairs generally, "God" is being pushed more and more out of life, losing more and more ground'.[3]

What is the Christian to do about this? For many, the tack to take is that of questioning all of humanity's advances, and trying to ensure that humans will not, in fact, take leave of God, but will once again be brought to the place of dependence upon God. Often, this takes the form of questioning the findings of the sciences in order to maintain a place for God. Bonhoeffer, however, rejects this approach. The reason for this, he says, is threefold:

> The attack by Christian apologetic on the adulthood of the world I consider to be in the first place pointless, in the second, ignoble, and the third place unchristian. Pointless, because it seems to me like an attempt to put a grown-up man back into adolescence, i.e. to make him dependent on things on which he is, in fact, no longer dependent, and thrusting him into problems that are, in fact, no longer problems, to him. Ignoble, because it amounts to an attempt to exploit man's weakness for purposes that are alien to him and to which he has not freely assented. Unchristian, because it confuses Christ with one particular stage in man's religiousness, i.e. with a human law.[4]

Bonhoeffer clearly is uninterested in any apologetic approach to Christianity that won't take seriously the fact that humanity has come of age. His question, then, is not 'how do we convince humanity that it is not of age?' Instead, he proposes: 'The question is: Christ and the world come of age'.[5] Bonhoeffer recognizes that the world has come of age; his approach in light of this is to ask how to proclaim Jesus Christ to the world that has come of age, and not try to run it down in its worldliness and try to convince it that it really isn't of age.

We're in danger of getting ahead of ourselves. Much of this discussion raises issues that we will deal with later: the kind of God who confronts the world come of age, and the kind of Christianity necessary in this historical setting. For now, we need to address the question of Bonhoeffer's theology of the world. His interest in and interpretation of the world and of Christ's relationship to the world are embedded in a deeper theology of creation that is the main focus of this chapter. Bonhoeffer sees the worldliness of the world as something to be celebrated, but his celebration of the world must be understood from the perspective of his theology of creation. Bonhoeffer gives such careful attention to the history of the world and its autonomy exactly because of his high view of God's creation and its place in God's work. The center of Bonhoeffer's theology of worldliness is, unsurprisingly, Jesus Christ. Jesus is the indicator that God is deeply concerned with his creation and that God has given the creation a life of its own. God is the creator, and so sovereign over the creation, but, as we will see, this isn't inconsistent with a high view of the creation and an appreciation for the fact that the creation is different than God and so needs to be respected as such.

WORLDLINESS IN THE EARLY BONHOEFFER

Bonhoeffer's appreciation for the creation is seen clearly in his early theology. In this section, we will analyze Bonhoeffer's theology of worldliness as seen in the late 1920s through an engagement of a text we have already engaged, *Act and Being*, and through a paper he gave while serving as a pastoral assistant in Barcelona. We turn first to the speech in Barcelona.

Barcelona

In 1928, Bonhoeffer served his curacy in a German speaking church in Barcelona. During this time we can see Bonhoeffer's conception of the creation and so his strong emphasis on worldliness developing. In this section, I will describe this development through an analysis of a speech Bonhoeffer gave to his Barcelona congregation entitled, 'Basic Questions of a Christian Ethic'.[6] While this text is concerned with ethics, as we have already seen, we cannot parse out Bonhoeffer's theology from his ethics; they are part and parcel. And, it is critical to grasp that Bonhoeffer's ethics is embedded in his theology of creation.

Bonhoeffer's interest in worldliness is seen from the beginning of this lecture. His opening line states, 'In speaking today about basic questions of a Christian ethic, we do not intend to embark on the . . . attempt to present universally valid Christian norms and commandments applicable to contemporary ethical questions. We intend instead to examine . . . the particular movement of ethical problems in today's world from the perspective of basic Christian ideas'.[7] This opening salvo indicates clearly that Bonhoeffer is not concerned with an ethics that attempts to enunciate universal norms detached from the concrete world. He is convinced that 'ethics is a matter of blood and a matter of history. It did not simply descend to earth from heaven. Rather, it is a child of the earth.'[8] What is clear from his opening words, and will continue to be clear throughout Bonhoeffer's ethical development, is that he is unwilling to approach ethics in an ahistorical way, in the same way he is unwilling to deal with revelation in an ahistorical way, as we will see in the following section. How does this play out in this lecture?

For Bonhoeffer, Christian ethics is not about principles, but about relationship to God. If one could establish universal norms or principles, then one could be ethical in a way that is completely separate from fellowship with God. It is this attempt to establish universal norms and principles that Bonhoeffer attacks when he writes bluntly, 'There is no Christian ethic'.[9] Bonhoeffer means by this that Christian ethics will have nothing to do with universal principles because 'there are no ethical principles enabling Christians, as it were, to make themselves moral'.[10] The ethic revealed in the story of the Scriptures has nothing to do with Christians making themselves moral through adherence to universal norms and principles. The inevitable result of this tack, as Bonhoeffer will painfully come to see in the church struggle of the 1930s, is a disengagement with the world and a separation of the church and her morality from the reality of the concrete world and all its ethical dilemmas. Bonhoeffer's burgeoning interest in Christian ethics, an ethics that is determined by the particularity of the incarnate Jesus Christ, will push him toward a conception of Christianity that is engaged with the world.

Bonhoeffer ends this lecture by rehearsing the legend of Antaeus, a giant who was stronger than any human on earth. Antaeus could not be defeated as long as he had both feet planted firmly on the earth. However, his strength left him if his adversary was able to lift him off the earth. Bonhoeffer uses this legend to make the following point: 'Those who would abandon the earth, who would flee the crisis of the present, will lose all the power still sustaining them by means of eternal, mysterious powers. The earth remains our mother just as God remains our father, and only those who remain true to their mother are placed into the father's arms'.[11] This is a striking statement, the import of which will only become obvious in Bonhoeffer's last days: the one who follows God and is faithful to the father is the one who doesn't look away from the earth, but remains true to the earth. 'Antanaean' becomes a symbol for Bonhoeffer for the 'indefatigable love of the earth' that should mark the followers of Jesus Christ.[12] This early lecture clearly demonstrates Bonhoeffer's developing sense of the earthly/worldly nature of Christianity.

Act and Being

In turning to *Act and Being*, our focus is on the way in which this book advances Bonhoeffer's developing interest in the worldly. This can be seen primarily through an analysis of Bonhoeffer's conception of revelation, contrasting this to the doctrine of revelation that was being worked out in Karl Barth's early theology, which Bonhoeffer had been reading and by which he was greatly influenced. We were introduced in Chapter 2 above to Bonhoeffer's critique of the way that Barth's early theology of revelation left the world seemingly untouched by God's revelation, due to Barth's desire to protect God's freedom. In his own presentation of a theology of revelation, Bonhoeffer adopts Barth's emphasis on divine freedom, but redefines that freedom in order to recast revelation as that which truly enters into and encounters human created existence. We will once again take up this theme here in order to analyze Bonhoeffer's focus on the 'concreteness' of revelation, which will show us more clearly Bonhoeffer's developing interest in worldliness.

In his book, *Reclaiming Dietrich Bonhoeffer*, Charles Marsh investigates the case that Bonhoeffer brings against Karl Barth's early actualistic conception of divine revelation. Barth's primary concern in his early theology is to protect the freedom of God, which he asserts has been lost in German liberalism, as God has been domesticated, made to be an object of human knowing instead of being the subject who freely reveals Himself to humans. Barth's early theology is clearly concerned with reestablishing the category of divine revelation, and thereby challenging the epistemological assumption of liberalism. However, though he is in favor of Barth's project, Bonhoeffer disagrees with the way Barth establishes the freedom of God's revelation over against the human creature.

There are significant implications of Bonhoeffer's critique of Barth for understanding Bonhoeffer's theology of creation. We have seen that for Barth, 'Revelation's paradox is its exploding into time and history without becoming part of time and history; its eternal contradictoriness'.[13] The result of this is a theology of revelation in which God reveals himself in history but God's revelation never becomes a part of concrete history. This clearly raises some questions regarding Barth's view of history and his attendant view of the creation. For Bonhoeffer, Barth's theology of revelation minimizes history, a move that Bonhoeffer feels is unfaithful to the Biblical testimony of God as creator and redeemer of the creation. As Marsh writes, '[Bonhoeffer] concludes that the conception of revelation configured strictly in terms of the act of God's freedom short-circuits the full reality of the world and splinter selfhood and community into discrete events of divine decision'.[14] Bonhoeffer is deeply concerned in *Act and Being* to establish the worldliness of God's revelation in such a way that it takes seriously the 'full reality of the world'.

Here we come to an important point for our understanding of worldliness in *Act and Being*: the relationship between revelation and, to use Marsh's term from above, the 'full reality of the world'. Bonhoeffer's uneasiness with Barth's proposal is located in the fact that Barth's view of revelation does not do justice to the reality of the world, the world that is God's creation and the world to which God is revealing himself. Bonhoeffer senses in Barth's actualism a denial of the reality of the world and the full entry of God into the world in the incarnation. As such, his own counter-proposal in *Act and Being* will center on God's self-revelation in Jesus Christ and his relation to the reality of the world. He will do this by once again employing the formula 'Christ existing as community', to which we were introduced in the last chapter.

How does the concept 'Christ existing as community' answer the question of God's revelation and its historical reality? How does it speak to the *being* of revelation, but do so in such a way that takes up the advances in Barth's early theology? To understand Bonhoeffer's proposal, we must look for a moment at his critique of two particular ways in which the being of revelation has been presented: the Roman Catholic conception of the Church and the Protestant orthodox conception of the Bible.

Bonhoeffer labels these views of revelation as 'institution'.[15] Both of these do exactly what Barth is against: they ossify revelation and make it an object of human knowing, thereby controllable by the human, and thus interfering with a true view of God's freedom. This means that God is bound to humans in such a way that God's revelation of himself is not free. The irony of this, however, is that even though revelation as institution affirms the being of revelation, these conceptions still ultimately leave the human existence untouched by revelation. There is still no true encounter with the God that reveals himself, just as in the case of Barthian actualism. It is important to note that, though he is critical of these two conceptions of revelation, Bonhoeffer affirms the impulse in each, against Barth, to see revelation as having entered into the 'full reality of the world'. His critique is of the way in which the being of revelation is conceived by these two viewpoints. The danger here is that, while in Barth revelation is too strictly conceived as act, in Roman Catholicism and Protestant orthodoxy, revelation is too strictly conceived as being. Bonhoeffer wants instead to speak of the way in which God's free act of revelation can be conceived of having true being in the world, as truly entering into and being at home in the concrete reality of the world and of human existence, and yet still remaining the act of God.

'Christ existing as community' is the way in which Bonhoeffer conceives of the freedom of God's revelation and its ability to enter the 'full reality of the world'. Bonhoeffer does this through a notion of freedom that will be important in our next section on *Creation and Fall.* Bonhoeffer's divergence from Barth is best understood, I suggest, as a difference in what it means for God to be free.[16] As we have seen, for Barth, God's freedom revolves around his conception of God's act: for God to be free is for God to be pure act and therefore to not have true being in the world. However, this leaves open the question of the connection between God and the history to which he reveals himself.

But where is God to be found? Where is he 'haveable, graspable'? Where does his revelation exist? Having rejected the ontological status of revelation conceived by the Roman Catholic and Orthodox Protestant conceptions of the being of revelation, Bonhoeffer asserts that the way to understanding the being of communion is through his formula 'Christ existing as community'. 'Christ existing as community' demonstrates that God cannot be conceived merely in his freedom from humanity, but only truly in his freedom for humanity. This statement, however, contains within it a conception of freedom that will become an important piece for understanding Bonhoeffer's view of the creaturely, both the human creature and the non-human creation. Human freedom is derived from God's freedom. What then is God's freedom? Marsh writes, '[F]or Bonhoeffer "Christ existing as community" is the way God shows himself as one whose freedom is in his binding, because God in Christ Jesus is one who really steps out of himself into the world without losing himself or relinquishing his identity'.[17] This bound freedom is not a necessity for God; he has freely chosen to be free as the one who is bound. He has entered truly into the world, and in doing so has freely chosen to be bound to it. His revelation, then, takes a particular form, the form of the community of the church, the Body of Christ. 'Thus, revelation is located neither in a novel occurrence of the past, in an event which has no direct connection with my old or new existence, nor in the always free and nonobjective divine acts';[18] Instead, 'revelation happens within and as the personal communion'.[19]

Bonhoeffer makes the connection between revelation and the church to be integral; in fact, for him, revelation and church are inseparable. We read, 'Revelation should be thought of only in reference to the concept of the church.'[20] The reason that Bonhoeffer makes such a strong connection between revelation and church is that for him it is only in conceiving of this relation that one can come to a true understanding of the relationship between act and being. Revelation is an activity of God that has real ontological status in history, in the concrete. 'Christ existing as community' is the unity of act and being. With Barth, Bonhoeffer conceives of revelation as an event, an 'occurrence' that happens in the present. As such, revelation is activity. But it is also being, an event that truly happens in history and gains ontological status in history. The being of revelation, however, is not the hierarchy of the Roman Church or the book of Scripture, but the community of faith. Christ is present as God's revelation in and through the community of faith. Bonhoeffer writes, '. . . God reveals the divine self in the church as a person. The community of faith is God's final revelation as "Christ existing as community", ordained for the end time of the world until the return of Christ. Here Christ has come in the closest proximity to humanity.'[21] This last sentence very clearly reveals the concern of Bonhoeffer to assert the historicity of Christ's presence. God's revelation does not keep aloof from history. He truly enters into it. And this entering is not merely a one-time entering in the earthly life of Christ. Instead, Bonhoeffer's conception of 'Christ existing as community' drives his theology in the direction of the continually present Christ, an emphasis that we saw in the Christology lectures when Bonhoeffer makes the critical methodological move to begin with the *Christus praesens*. As such, the church is the place of the unity of act and being.[22] Bonhoeffer's claim is that 'the being of revelation "is", rather, the being of the community of persons that is constituted and formed by the person of Christ.'[23]

'Christ existing as community' is the way that Bonhoeffer overcomes the lack of historicity of revelation in Barth and the lack of freedom of revelation in the ontological theories of revelation he has critiqued. Here he finds the basis for continuity of revelation: continuity is not to be found in the individual human subject, but in the subject of Christ, who is present and exists in and as the community. He is revealed in the social relations of the community.[24] He is the one who is free, and yet also bound to the particular historical community of the church. In the Christ who is present in the church community we have the convergence of the freedom of God's act and the historical being of revelation.

In bringing this section to a close, we can summarize what we have learned in this way: in *Act and Being*, Bonhoeffer takes a huge step toward his thoughts on worldliness that will come to fruition in the prison letters. In his concern to assert that God has revealed himself by entering 'the full reality of the world' Bonhoeffer has set the foundation for the conviction that will grow over time that the Christian is one who also enters into 'the full reality of the world' because the Christian follows Christ, who fully entered. There is a convergence in *Act and Being* of Christ, the church, and the world that will continue to unfold in Bonhoeffer's theology.

Having explored these two early texts, and having identified the importance in each for understanding Bonhoeffer's early commitment to 'worldliness', we will now turn to *Creation and Fall* to see Bonhoeffer's development of a more full-orbed theology of creation.

WORLDLINESS IN *CREATION AND FALL*

Creation and Fall reveals Bonhoeffer's continuing desire to set forth an understanding of Christianity that is grounded in the earthly. In this text, Bonhoeffer explicates the first three chapters of Genesis, emphasizing the goodness of the world as created by God.

Bonhoeffer begins this text, unsurprisingly, with an emphasis on the need of humans for the revelation of God in his Word. It is this Word, and this Word alone, that binds the Creator and the creature. There is no necessity of creation; there is nothing in God that must create and there is therefore no ontologically necessary point of contact between God and the creation. There is only relationship that God has himself established: His presence in and to the creation through his Word. This is part and parcel of Bonhoeffer's understanding of divine freedom as freedom for and not freedom from. God's freedom is to be understood only in so far as he has used his freedom to bind himself to the world through the speaking of his Word. As such, it is in understanding that there is not a necessity for God to create that both the Creator and the creation are free. The Creator is the one who creates in freedom, and who is present to the creation through his freely given Word. The creation is free in that it is the creature of the free Creator, and is set free through obedience to God's Word. An important emphasis in the early pages of *Creation and Fall* is the emphasis on the distinction between the Creator and the creation, a distinction that expresses the freedom of both.

God cannot be confused with the world. God, in his freedom, creates something other than God. He chooses, for reasons that we cannot fathom nor examine, to create. What he creates is not God. It is other, created with an integrity that is its own, and that gives it a freedom and a life that it would not have if it was merely an extension of God. Through this creation, the Creator is glorified and praised by the creation. The integrity of the creation is to be the creation of God, and thus to give him praise. Bonhoeffer writes, 'Not the created work, no, but the Creator wills to be glorified. The earth is formless and void, but the Creator is the Lord, the one who brings about the wholly new, the strange, inconceivable work of God's dominion and love'.[25] God creates in freedom, and in doing so is to be praised by the creation.

But the creation is also free. In creating the creation as something other than himself, God gives the creation its own integrity. In contrast to other creation myths, 'in which the deity imparts its own nature' and thus 'the creation itself is a portion of what belongs to God's very nature', the creation story of Genesis affirms the distinction of God and creation.[26] This is not only an affirmation of the Creator's freedom, but also the creation's freedom: the creation is free to be the creation of the Creator. It is only in the fact that the creation is given its own being, and thus its own integrity to be other than God, that the creation can be free and achieve its ends of praising God. In doing this, 'the Creator enormously increases the power of the creation, by giving to creation its own being as that which has form. In this form creation exists over against God in a new way, and in existing over against God it wholly belongs to God'.[27]

What, then, is the connection between the Creator and the creation? It is not a common essence, a common nature, in which the created world shares in God's essence; instead, it is the Word of God. God's Word creates and binds God and world. God's creation is *good* because it is the result of God's good Word, of God's good will. God is *for* the world, and is oriented toward the world, in that he is present to and in the world through his Word of command. 'God says, God speaks. This means that God creates in complete freedom. Even in creating, God remains wholly free over against what is created. . . . God does not enter into what is created as its substance; instead what relates God to what is created is God's command'.[28] The mode of God's presence in the world is his Word, his command. Just as in *Act and Being*, so here: God's revelation truly enters into the world. God is truly present in and to the world, but not through a confusion of the being of God with the being of the world, but through the distinction of God from the world, which thus protects the freedom of both God and world.

We have seen in this discussion Bonhoeffer's attempt to establish the integrity and importance of the world by establishing the freedom of God and world that exists only in their being bound together. Both have integrity, both are 'themselves'. Though God is not bound to the world by necessity, he has bound the world to himself by his freedom and grace. In binding the world to himself, he has made it free. As we turn now to the creation of the human, we will see these conceptions carry forward: the human is given created integrity and an existence of living in the freedom of being God's creature. However, just as the integrity of the world only exists in its being bound to God by his Word, so is the case with the human creature.

God creates the human in his image. But there are so many differing opinions of what *imago dei* means; what does it mean for Bonhoeffer? To put it simply, for the creature to be created in the image of God is for the creature to be free. Up until the point of his creation of the human in the creation story, God has not created his image on earth. In the creation of the human, this image is established on earth. In creating the human, God creates his image in the community of the male and female. Consequently, it is in the relationship between male and female, in the community of the human, that God can behold the image of himself. But what does it mean to image God? What is the content of this idea?

For Bonhoeffer, to image God is to be free. But this raises a question: how can that which is creature, that which is conditioned by nature, be free? In what way can we say that the human is free when the human is created to worship and be obedient to God? The answer to this is that it is precisely in this obedience that the creature is free. The creature is created to be bound by the command of God, and by the other. Freedom, Bonhoeffer asserts, is freedom for others: 'How is the creature free? The creature is free in that one creature exists in relation to another creature, in that one human being is free for another human being'.[29]

This emphasis on human freedom directs us to the earthly nature of human being. The human is only free when the human lives in relational unity with her surroundings. To be a free human is to recognize the limitation of humanity due to its being conditioned by its bodily life, and by others. To be human is to be bound. To be human is to be free within the boundaries given to humanity by God. As such, these boundaries exist for the sake of human flourishing. God's commands exist to guide the human into the life he gave to them. When God commands Adam and Eve in the garden, he does so for the sake of their flourishing. He tells them to eat of any tree except the tree of the knowledge of good and evil. His commands are both positive and negative: eat, flourish, enjoy created life. But, do not eat of this tree because in doing so you transgress your boundaries and cease to be free. God binds the human to his Word in order that the human might be free.

It follows from this that the human is free only in being free to exist within the world and only in its God-given role as steward of the world. In being bound to God and to one another, the human takes on the role of steward of God's earth. The human is called to exercise this role not as one who uses and abuses the earth but as one who recognizes her essential relationship to the earth. In creating the human, God took the dust of the earth and breathed life into it, thus creating Adam. As a result, Bonhoeffer deems it proper to refer to the earth as the mother of humankind. Accordingly, the human role of stewardship is not a role of domination, but of tender care. So, humanity is to rule over the earth for the sake of the flourishing of both the human and the earth.

For Bonhoeffer, then, there is no flight from body, no dualism, no 'spiritualizing' of humanity. Humanity is a union of heaven and earth and can only exist in its integrity by being properly related to both heaven and earth. It is only when humans exist as worldly beings that God is honored. A view of humanity that seeks to free the creature from the world by viewing creaturely existence as 'heavenly' or 'otherworldly' is not consistent with the Biblical view of God's creation intention. A desire to escape the earth is to enslave the human. Only humanity who recognizes her worldliness can properly live out the command of God and experience the freedom that God desires for his human creation.

We move now to Bonhoeffer's notion of worldliness in his *Ethics*. We saw above in Bonhoeffer's lecture in Barcelona that ethics is always a concrete response to God's command and never a system of preconceived principles. Bonhoeffer accused the church of the 1930s of falling into the universalizing trap of principled ethics by which it kept itself at a distant from the true demands of ethics in opposition to the Nazi's. Instead of engaging in true resistance to Nazism, the church (both the German Christians and the Confessing Church) fell back into the safety of principles, and thereby failed to truly follow Christ into the difficulties of the fallen world. A church that understands ethics as principles will inevitably fail to take seriously the problems of the world. But, as we have seen so far in this chapter, this is not an option for Bonhoeffer. Because of his theology of creation, Bonhoeffer's ethics must be deeply engaged in the concrete world. There is no option for hiding behind principles and so remaining aloof from the life of God's creation, no matter how difficult and confusing it might be to engage it in the name of Christ. Jesus did not stand aloof from the world, but entered into it with all its confusion, and so would the one who takes seriously God's creation and his work to redeem that creation.

WORLDLINESS IN *ETHICS*

In turning to *Ethics*, we do so with the emphasis on the created world that we have been investigating in this chapter. For Bonhoeffer, ethical life is a life of engagement with the real world in concrete ways. While this emphasis on ethical engagement with a concrete focus is found throughout the book, my focus in this section will be on three particular emphases found therein. First, we will briefly explore Bonhoeffer's assertion that Christ *is* reality, once again making clear the connection between Christology and worldliness. Second, we will engage Bonhoeffer's essay 'Natural Life', considering Bonhoeffer's proposal for a Protestant ethic that takes seriously the natural, something that, in his estimation, has been lacking in theologies of the Reformation tradition. Finally, we will investigate Bonhoeffer's theology of the mandates to see their place in Bonhoeffer's worldly ethics.

We begin by exploring Bonhoeffer's understanding of Christ as reality. The concept of reality appears at the very beginning of *Ethics*, in the opening essay, 'Christ, Reality and Good'. Bonhoeffer is here concerned with enunciating an ethics that is concerned with reality, not with principles and rules that take us away from reality. What this means, then, is that ethics cannot be first and foremost concerned with the reality of the ethicist nor the reality of the world but must be concerned with living in fellowship with Jesus Christ, who is the ultimate reality. More than this, it is about the reality of Christ becoming real in the world, or, to use his language from *Sanctorum Communio*, about the actualization in history of the realized Christ. To be ethical, then, is not simply to do ethical things or to behave in a certain way. To be ethical is to have the form of Christ take form in oneself, and thus to become a partaker of the ultimate reality, Jesus Christ. Christ, as the center of all, *is* the shape of the ethical life.

This directly impacts our understanding of the good. Good is not an abstract concept or a construction of human intellect or morals. To be good is to be conformed to the image of Jesus Christ: 'the question of the good become the question of participating in God's reality revealed in Jesus Christ'.[30] Bonhoeffer contrasts this way of defining good and reality in opposition to both Reinhold Niebuhr and the 'positive-empiricist' approach.[31] The problem with both of these approaches is that they separate the good from the real, and thus make 'good' to be a value statement about different states of reality.

Some reality is good, some is bad. However, Bonhoeffer counters, the good and the real can never be separated, and *both* are defined solely by the revelation of Jesus Christ, the one who is the good and the real. When Christian ethics speaks of the good and the real, then,

> It means thereby the reality of God as the ultimate reality beyond and in all that exists. It means also the reality of the existing world that is real only through the reality of God. The reality of God is not just another idea. Christian faith perceives this in the fact that the reality of God has revealed itself and witnessed to itself in the middle of the real world. In Jesus Christ, the reality of God has entered into the reality of this world.[32]

Let's look closely at this important paragraph. When Christianity claims to speak of reality, it speaks first of God, but also includes the world, an emphasis that is consistent with *Creation and Fall*. Jesus Christ as the only true reality does not exclude, but includes, the creation. Jesus Christ is the person in whom the reality of God has revealed itself and witnessed to itself, but the revelation of this person who is reality has been revealed in a particular place: *in the middle of the real world.* Christ, the reality and the good, is the revelation of God, not in some distant domain, not as a word that is trumpeted from transcendence but that never encounters human reality, but in the midst of the world. Jesus is the reality and the good. Thus, for the world to live in reality is for the world to live in Jesus, to be conformed to his image.

Hence, the very notion of ethics takes on a different flavor. Ethics is not about valuation of good and evil and making correct choices based on our own competence in discerning the correct path. Ethics, instead, is about living in the reality of Jesus Christ. Later, in the essay entitled 'History and Good [1]', Bonhoeffer writes, 'Good is the action in accordance with Jesus Christ; *action in accordance with Christ is action in accord with reality'*.[33] We can see here Bonhoeffer overcoming the tendency in many ethical systems to avoid engagement with the world. When it is believed that Christ is at the center of the world, at the center of human experience, history, and nature, at the center of all true relationships, and that Christ is the reality of all, then an ethic is envisaged that focuses not on theoretical questions of good and evil but on participating in the reality of Christ in his engagement with the world. In *Ethics*, Bonhoeffer is less concerned with working out rules and principles because he knows that these take us away from reality, and far more concerned with actions that are in accordance with Christ, and thus are engaged with reality. An 'ethic of Jesus' is unnecessary; a code that is derived from the life of Jesus and applied to history is an abstraction. What matters is participating in the activity of the present Christ, and so living in reality.

In this, we see very clearly the connection between Jesus, the world, and ethics. These cannot be thought apart from one another. Bonhoeffer's Christology, theology of creation, and ethics all combine to emphasize the importance of taking the world very seriously exactly because it is God's creation and because of his love for the world. Let's continue to explore Bonhoeffer's *Ethics* and its connection to worldliness by looking at his essay entitled 'Natural Life', in which he proposes an approach to an ethic of natural life that is missing from the vast majority of Protestant ethical teaching.

Bonhoeffer begins 'Natural Life' with the following comment: 'The concept of the natural has fallen into disrepute in Protestant ethics. For some theologians it was completely lost in the darkness of general sinfulness, whereas for others too on the brightness of primal creation. Both were grave misuses that led to the elimination of the category of the natural from Protestant thought'.[34] Bonhoeffer bemoans this lack of attention to the natural in Protestant thought exactly because it leaves Protestant ethics disconnected from the issues of natural life. He believes this is due to a misunderstanding of grace and sin. For Protestant theologians, whose emphasis is on the need for grace due to sin, any discussion of the natural is in danger of losing a strong emphasis on grace. Bonhoeffer states, 'Confronted with the light of grace, everything human and natural sank into the night of sin.'[35] Because the natural life of the human in the fallen world is lost in darkness, Protestant thought no longer sought to give direction to human life in the world, asserting grace but giving no guidance to natural life. For Protestant theology, 'God's word condemned the natural and the unnatural alike. That meant complete dissolution in the sphere of natural life.'[36] Clearly, this will not do for Bonhoeffer. His whole theology leads him against the stream of Protestant ethics that condemn the natural in the name of sin and grace. In his estimation, 'the concept of the natural must be recovered from the gospel itself'.[37] The failure of Protestant ethics has meant a failure to grasp the gospel. God did not come merely to condemn the world, but to heal it. God has not given up on the natural life that he created, but has given himself for it. As such, Bonhoeffer cannot be content to carry on the tradition of Protestant ethics, but offers a counter-proposal in which the created world is taken very seriously.

However, we must be careful not to assume that Bonhoeffer, in his rejection of Protestant ethics, likewise rejects the Protestant theology of sin and grace. We have seen clearly in this book that Bonhoeffer takes seriously a theology of sin that leaves humans in deep need of God's grace in Jesus Christ. Bonhoeffer's difference from classic Protestant ethics lies not in the fact that he rejects Protestant theologies doctrines of sin and grace, but in a distinction he makes between the created and the natural. To this difference we now turn.

For Bonhoeffer, the natural is not to be simplistically identified with the created. This was the error that Protestant theology made. Instead, Bonhoeffer suggests that the created is that which existed before the fall, while the natural is that which exists after the fall. This means that the natural is the world that is preserved by God as it waits for Jesus Christ. Or, in Bonhoeffer's words, 'The natural is that which, after the fall, is directed toward the coming of Jesus Christ'.[38] This provides Bonhoeffer with the necessary schema by which to take seriously both the fallenness of the world and the importance of the natural. Sin doesn't destroy God's work in creation. It deeply effects the created world, as we have seen, but God, in his grace, continues to uphold the world by preserving it. As such, the world, though fallen, cannot 'sink into the night of sin' but must be engaged by a Protestant theology that takes seriously God's work of redemption. The natural is fallen, but is upheld by God. Bonhoeffer is clear that the natural cannot be thought of apart from the work of God in Christ to uphold and preserve it to the time when God will overcome sin and restore the created. In examining the failure of Protestant ethics, Bonhoeffer focuses on the loss of the ultimate and the penultimate, a dialectic he describes in the essay that precedes 'Natural Life'.

Bonhoeffer describes the ultimate as the justification of the sinner by grace. Justification is the work by which God, through his justifying word of forgiveness, sets people free from sin and for life with God and neighbor. In the justifying work of God, 'past sin has been sunk into the depths of God's love in Jesus Christ and overcome; the future will be, without sin, a life born of God'.[39] Through the justification of the sinner, the past is overcome and the future is assured. However, this doesn't make the future a present reality. It is true, but it is not yet so. Life in the present, in the penultimate, in anchored in the life, death and resurrection of Jesus Christ, and so lives 'because of and toward the living, dying, and rising of Jesus Christ', but the attainment of the future life is not yet ours.[40] The future life of freedom from sin is the ultimate; life as one who is forgiven and justified, but who does not yet have the totality of the future life, is penultimate. And it is in *this* time, the penultimate, that the justified sinner lives, by faith toward the ultimate.

Penultimate life, then, is the time of waiting for the ultimate justifying word of God. This is 'a time of God's permission, waiting, and preparation.'[41] In other words, the penultimate is identified with the natural. We have seen that the natural is the time after the fall that is upheld by God on the way to the coming of Jesus Christ. This is the same thing as the penultimate: a time of waiting and preparation for the coming of Jesus Christ. The natural does not have ontological existence from itself; it is given its existence by God's grace. Similarly, the penultimate cannot be understood from within itself but must be understood in its relation to the ultimate. The penultimate is the time in which we now live, even though it only exists as superseded by the ultimate. Life in the penultimate cannot be abandoned, but it is also only truly understood in its relation to the ultimate.

This discussion allows us to better grasp Bonhoeffer's critique of Protestant ethics: it sought to live based solely on the ultimate and so divorced itself from life in the penultimate, from natural life. It sought to live in the ultimate instead of realizing God's will for life in the penultimate. The danger of flight from the present lurks in Christianity; Bonhoeffer proposes that Christianity is best understood not as a flight from the present world, but as deeply emerged in the present world. But, the Christian knows that the present world isn't ultimate, and therefore won't allow the terms of the world to dictate her living. Living by a faith anchored in God's ultimate word of justification, the Christian can live freely in the natural, penultimate world, taking seriously the issues of the fallen world and offering answers to the questions that plague the natural, fallen world.

Bonhoeffer's understanding of the penultimate/natural means that in his ethics, this world and its problems are taken with great seriousness. Though the world is fallen, it is upheld by God, and is directed toward the coming of Jesus Christ, for which it waits, whether it knows it or not. The penultimate world is fallen, but this doesn't mean that it should be lost in the night of sin; rather, it must be taken with seriousness by those who know that the natural is not the ultimate. With the penultimate/ultimate dialectic, Bonhoeffer believes he has provided a theological rationale for taking seriously the natural in a way that Protestant ethics never has.

With this understanding of the natural in place, we turn now to Bonhoeffer's conception of the mandates. Traditional Lutheran theology developed the 'orders of creation', a theological conception that was used to express the way that God has structured creation for the sake of human living. In this interpretation of the orders of creation, God has created hierarchical structures by which he gives human life order. The orders in Lutheran theology include marriage and family, government, labor, and ministry. These structures are viewed as part of God's original creation, given by him from the beginning as the created good for human life. As Lutheran theology continued to develop, the orders came to be seen as means of God's revelation. This became problematic in Bonhoeffer's time as the Nazis used the ideology of the orders to claim that they were the means through which God was revealing his will for Germany. Because government is an order of creation, given by God as the means by which he orders society, the Nazis made the claim that they were the revelation of God's will.

Because of this, Bonhoeffer believes that the traditional conception of the orders of creation in Lutheran theology needs to be reexamined. Bonhoeffer critiques the traditional conception of the orders in *Ethics* through his notion of the mandates. Bonhoeffer believed that the fatal error of the traditional idea of the orders is that they are too easily divorced from God's revelation in Jesus Christ. In other words, the orders are vulnerable to abuse because they are positioned as independent means of revelation that are embedded in creation. As such, the orders can be easily divorced from Christ, and used just as the Nazis used them, to justify human ideologies by claiming that these have the status of being revelation from God.

Bonhoeffer makes two alterations to the traditional teaching on the orders with his conception of the mandates. First, he writes that the mandates are not embedded in creation, but are instead put in place by God *after* the fall, as ways that God is preserving the world while it awaits the final revelation of Jesus Christ. This move is connected to the second key distinction between the mandates and the orders: for Bonhoeffer, the orders are thoroughly Christocentric.

In opposition to the orders of creation, which become means through which structures which are independent of Jesus Christ are set in place, for Bonhoeffer, the mandates are the way that the *concrete command of Jesus Christ* comes to humans, and this commandment 'embraces . . . all of human life'.[42] The commandment of God that sets humans free for life comes to humans in four forms: the church, marriage and family, culture, and government. None of these are independent of God's special revelation in Jesus Christ; this was the error of Lutheran theologians' emphasis on orders of creation. Neither is God's commandment to be found anywhere other than where God authorizes it, and this is in the mandates.

Bonhoeffer defines mandate as follows: 'the concrete divine commission grounded in the revelation of Christ and the testimony of Scripture; it is the authorization and legitimization to declare a particular divine commandment, the conferring of divine authority on an earthly institution'.[43] The mandates are the means by which God has taken up certain earthly (i.e. natural, because fallen) institutions and made them to be bearers of his command in Jesus Christ, the command for life. God wills that the creature live creaturely life; though the world is fallen, God remains committed to establishing his creation in the life he created it to live. During the time of the natural, the mandates are the means by which God commands his creatures to live. These mandates are not grounded in the world; they come to the world from God and give structure to that world that would otherwise be chaotic. The mandates reveal the love that God has for the world, and are the means by which God expresses his authority in the world.

It is essential for our purposes in this chapter to see how the mandates emphasize the importance of the creation in Bonhoeffer's theology. The mandates are the means by which God makes humans free to live in the natural world. Though fallen, the world is not lost. The mandates are the divine grace of providing sustaining order to a world which would otherwise fall into darkness. While Bonhoeffer takes sin very seriously, he takes God's command and his grace even more seriously. One does not have to be a professional ethicist to know how to live in this world; one simply needs to live life according to the commandment of Christ through the divine mandates. This is the promotion of life even in the midst of death, and it indicates Bonhoeffer's theological appropriation of the philosophy of life, a movement in the late 19th and early 20th centuries whose best-known proponents were Friedrich Nietzsche and Wilhelm Dilthey. Nietzsche, of course, railed against Christianity as a life-draining religion that was ultimately about controlling the masses and maintaining power in society. Against this, Nietzsche argued powerfully that any true creed must set humans free for life. He desired to do this with his well-known conception of the *Übermensch*, the 'superman'. Bonhoeffer takes up the challenge of these critiques, desiring himself to show forth a Christianity that is life-affirming.

The mandates are one of his key arguments in this attempt. God's command is a command for the creature to live. This is true from the very beginning of Scripture, when God commands Adam and Eve to eat and be fruitful. The commands of God embrace and encourage humans to live fully the created life given to them by God. With the mandates, Bonhoeffer expresses a Christ-centered, life affirming theology of the earthly. Because God has become human, humans are free to live earthly, concrete lives, without apology and without a dualism between heaven and earth. As with Antaeus in the lecture in Barcelona, so here in *Ethics*: to be human is to live with both feet firmly planted on earth. This is the will of God.

THE WORLD COME OF AGE

We return now to the organizing theme of this chapter: the world come of age. Throughout this chapter, we have examined Bonhoeffer's theology of creation and the strong sense of the earthly/worldly that marks his thought. We bring this emphasis with us as we return to Bonhoeffer's thoughts on worldliness in the prison letters.

The first important point to make regarding Bonhoeffer's conception of the world come of age is to understand that this is not a statement that the world is becoming better through some immanent evolutionary force. In our investigation of the natural and the penultimate, it became clear that Bonhoeffer does not see any dichotomy between the fallenness of the world and an affirmation of the world. God has created the world, and though it has rebelled against him and rejected him as Lord, God has acted to uphold to preserve his creation as it awaits the final work of God to return it to his intention. This world is not as God intended it to be, but it is God's world, and his will for it maintains through the incarnation of Christ and his work to redeem the whole created world, and not just the souls of individual humans. So, though Bonhoeffer affirms the coming of age of the world, this is not a declaration that the world is becoming better through its own immanent forces. Instead, Bonhoeffer's recognition that the world has come of age is a statement about the condition of the natural world and a call for the church to recognize this in order to be positioned to proclaim the Lordship of Christ in this place.

We read above Bonhoeffer's judgment that Christian apologetics that tries to return the world come of age to a pre-pubescent form is unchristian; the reason for this should now be plain. Because of Bonhoeffer's theology of creation, one must understand the world and take it very seriously, not for its own sake, but for the sake of Christ and his relation to the world. When the church fails to adequately understand the world, she is in great danger of flight from the problems and sufferings of the world. When Protestant ethics allows the natural life of humans to be lost in the darkness of sin, this is indicative of a theology that doesn't take creation seriously. This can never be Bonhoeffer's approach. Because of his Christology, because of God's entry into the world in created from in order to bind up creation and restore it, Bonhoeffer can never be content to judge the fallen world lost in sin; it is lost in sin, but this isn't the ultimate word about the world. The ultimate word is God's word of justification in Jesus Christ, and because this word is ultimate it must shape the life of the church as it lives in and engages life in the penultimate. Bonhoeffer takes the world come of age seriously, not because the world come of age can understand and define itself with clarity, but because it can't, and it must hear the word of justification and the call to life that is the command of God given in Jesus Christ. Bonhoeffer takes the world come of age seriously because he takes Jesus Christ seriously.

But what are the implications of this for the church? Will the church acknowledge that the world has come of age and take seriously God's will for the creation, or will the church continue to try to force the world to see that it hasn't come of age, even though it has? What does our theme in this chapter say about the church in the time of the world come of age? The church follows after a God who became a human, thereby affirming life and calling people to true life. However, as we have discovered in our explorations of Bonhoeffer's theology, the God that the church follows is a God who went the way of suffering, the way of the cross. Bonhoeffer's theology of creation and his emphasis on worldliness as a Christian theme brings us once again face to face with the suffering figure of Jesus Christ. God doesn't only enter into the fallen world, he suffers for it. The church, then, should be marked by the form of this suffering God as it lives in the penultimate while anchored in the ultimate.

In turning to our next chapter, we turn to an investigation of the suffering God who can help. We have laid the three foundation stones of Christ, church, and world in Bonhoeffer. Now, we turn to see his theology of the suffering God who engages the world, not at its point of weakness, but at its point of strength.

CHAPTER 5

ETSI DEUS NON DARETUR: LIVING WITHOUT GOD BEFORE GOD

Having outlined Bonhoeffer's conception of worldliness, we will now engage what is undoubtedly one of the most intriguing and difficult notions in the Bonhoeffer *corpus*, the notion of living life *etsi deus non daretur,* which can be best translated 'as if God did not exist'. This chapter follows on from the last: there, we saw that Bonhoeffer has a high view of the world, and a deep appreciation for it exactly because it is willed by God and he created the world, and the human within it, to live in freedom. Hence, for Bonhoeffer, there is an appropriate autonomy of the world, an autonomy that exists within the boundaries set for the world by God. However, when these boundaries are crossed, there is an inappropriate autonomy of the world, an autonomy in which God is no longer honored or worshipped as God, but is denied and despised. This rejection of God brings with it a great deal of misery as the world suffers under the weight of the rejection of her proper autonomy in order to establish herself in autonomy apart from God.

In this chapter I will explain the connection between Bonhoeffer's thoughts on *etsi deus non daretur* and the suffering of God, a connection that I feel is important and that hasn't been brought to the fore in Bonhoeffer studies generally. As we have seen at numerous places in this book, for Bonhoeffer, our vision of God must be grounded in his revelation of Himself, as must our life of obedience to the God so revealed. If this is the case, then, in what way does connecting *etsi deus non daretur* and the suffering God shape both our thinking about God and about the shape of life in the world come of age? The aim of this chapter is to demonstrate this connection, and to point us forward to our final chapter on Bonhoeffer's notion of religionless Christianity.

ETSI DEUS NON DARETUR: INTRODUCING THE THEME

In his letter of 16 July 1944, Bonhoeffer writes to Bethge regarding the concept *etsi deus non daretur*. The purpose of this discussion is to address the situation of the world that has come of age. Bonhoeffer begins his discussions on this by offering a brief sketch on the historical development of the West, and the way in which it has sought to set itself up to work *etsi deus non daretur*. In various disciplines, the philosophical, the political and the scientific, the need for God as a 'working hypothesis'[1] is no longer necessary, as so many things of the world can now be explained apart from him. Thinkers like Herbert of Cherbury in theology, Montaigne and Bodin in ethics, and Machiavelli in politics are invoked to demonstrate the way in which God is no longer needed as a hypothesis. Instead of needing to assert God in order to ground human morals or scientific investigation, it is now only necessary that we use our reason, or to understand and obey the universal law of morality that is inherent in us, or to organize the state in such a way that the good is served.

We have seen for Bonhoeffer that the movement of the Western world to a position that no longer needs God as a working hypothesis is not something to bemoan or to try to overturn. Instead, Bonhoeffer believes that 'For the sake of intellectual honesty, that working hypothesis should be dropped, or as far as possible eliminated'.[2] Bonhoeffer is aware of the repercussions from such 'intellectual honesty', as is clear by the following statement that follows in the letter: 'Anxious souls will ask what room there is left for God now'.[3] What room indeed? Is there a need for God at all? Now that the working hypothesis of Western Christianity has been dropped, does that mean that God has been dropped? This is what the 'death of God' theologians believed Bonhoeffer was saying. But is it?

It becomes clear as one reads the letter that Bonhoeffer is not here calling for a Nietzschean notion of the death of God. But he is doing something that, though perhaps not as radical as Nietzsche's 'God is dead', is nonetheless a significant challenge to Christian theology. He is calling for the death of the particular *idea of God* that sustained Western Christianity for much of her history: the God of power. For Bonhoeffer, the traditional view of God as a God of power is the *deus ex machina*,[4] the God who swoops in and rescues people in their time of need. Bonhoeffer's assertion, however, is that the God of power is not the God who is revealed in Jesus Christ. The God revealed in Christ is a God who suffers, who enters into the misery of humanity and in doing so is the God who helps. Bonhoeffer's vision of the weak God is clearly illustrated in his poem 'Christians and Pagans':

> People go to God in their need
> They pray to him for help, asking for fortune and bread
> For deliverance from sickness, debt, and death.
> All people do so, all, Christians and pagans.
> People go to God in his need,
> They find him poor, reviled, without shelter and bread,
> Overwhelmed by sin, weakness, and death.
> Christians stand by God in his suffering.
> God goes to all people in their need,
> Satisfying the body and the soul with his bread,
> For Christians and pagans he died the death on the cross,
> And forgives them both.[5]

In this poem, we have a wonderful synopsis of the God whom Bonhoeffer believes Christianity must find if it is going to move forward in a world come of age. While humanity goes to God in a search for power, those who come to the cross of Christ come to a God who is powerless, who has given himself over to his executioners, and who therefore is not the God that humans, both Christians and pagans, seek. But those who would realize that God is a God who suffers, and who therefore calls humans to stand by him in his suffering, come to the true God. When this God is recognized, then the true God who hangs on the cross and thus brings forgiveness to the humanity who would live without him can be sought for his help. But, because this is a particular kind of God, the help we receive from him is a particular kind of help. Bonhoeffer writes, 'Here is the decisive difference between Christianity and all religions. Man's religiosity makes him look in his distress to the power of God in the world. . . . The Bible directs man to God's powerlessness and suffering; only the suffering God can help.'[6]

In making these claims, Bonhoeffer is making a theological statement regarding the development of the notion of *etsi deus non daretur*. For Cherbury, Machiavelli et al., the desire is to create a world that can be run successfully without the working hypothesis of God. Bonhoeffer responds to this, not by fighting back and seeking to establish God as working hypothesis, but exactly by recognizing that the 'God' who is being rejected in the works of the above-mentioned thinkers is a metaphysical construct and not the God revealed in Jesus Christ. The metaphysical 'God' is not given; but God, in Jesus Christ, the God who suffers, can help. So Bonhoeffer writes,

> we cannot be honest unless we recognize that we have to live in the world *etsi deus non daretur.* And this is just what we recognize – before God! God himself compels us to recognize it. So our coming of age leads us to a true recognition of our situation before God. . . . The God who lets us live in the world without the working hypothesis of God is the God before whom we stand continually. Before God and with God we live without God.[7]

The connection between the suffering God and living life before God and without God is clearly seen here: the fact that God is a suffering God means that we must live our lives in a way that is 'without' him, but the him that we are without is the metaphysical 'God' of the tradition and not the Father of Jesus Christ. As such, we live without *that* 'God' but do so before the *true* God. Bonhoeffer's conception here is that we take leave of the 'God' of power to whom we have grown so accustomed, and bravely dare to live life in fellowship with the suffering God. Notice Bonhoeffer's definition of what is being rejected: 'the working hypothesis of God'. This is what the death of God theologians missed. In their mind, Bonhoeffer's invocation of *etsi deus non daretur* was of a piece with the notion that God is dead. However, it is quite clear that Bonhoeffer is not here speaking of the death of God, but of the death of the 'working hypothesis' of God. This has nothing to do with a denial of God and everything to do with the denial of the *deus ex machina.* The suffering God, who is truly God, and who remains Lord of all, is the God who 'lets us live in the world without the working hypothesis of God'; it is this God, the true God, 'before whom we continually stand'. Hence, it is only in making the connection between the suffering God and the life that he compels us to live, life *etsi deus non daretur*, that we can understand Bonhoeffer's startling claims in the prison letters.

In response to the anxious souls who would ask 'what room is there left for God?', Bonhoeffer says: the room on the cross. That is where God is to be found, in his weakness and suffering, and yet in that very weakness and suffering God forgives. 'God lets himself be pushed out of the world on the cross. He is weak and powerless in the world, and that is precisely the way, the only way, in which he is with us and helps us.'[8] God is to be found, but he may not be found where people expect to find him. This directs our attention to the cross of Christ as the locus of true thinking about God. The *deus ex machina* is a metaphysical invention of Western Christianity, of the phase of religion. This God is the God of the theology of glory, to use Luther's term. Luther counters the theology of glory with a theology of the cross, a theological method that seeks God not in his strength, but in the place where he is to be found, dying on the cross. Bonhoeffer follows Luther in this methodology, desiring to look to the suffering God as the one who can help. As such, we must turn our attention now to Bonhoeffer's theology of the suffering God, to see its development in Bonhoeffer's work and so to better be able to understand life *etsi deus non daretur*.

THE SUFFERING GOD IN THE CHRISTOLOGY LECTURES

As we turn our attention once again to the Christology lectures, we do so with a focus on Bonhoeffer's notion of the humiliated Christ found therein. In Chapter 2 we explored the epistemology of the Christology lectures through an investigation of the logos/Counter-Logos schema, identifying the proper Christological question to be the 'Who?' question. All other questions directed by Christ become the means by which the logos, fallen human reason, seeks to classify, and thereby evade, the Lordship of Christ. In the confrontation between the logos and the Counter-Logos, the only proper question of dethroned reason is 'Who are you? Are you God?'

But we also saw that Christ is not immediately recognizable as God. He is the God-man who is hidden 'in the likeness of sinful flesh'.[9] For Bonhoeffer, this changes the whole question of Christology. No longer is the primary Christology issue the relation of the two natures of Christ, but between the God-man and sinful human flesh. This becomes 'the central problem of Christology'.[10] The hiddenness of Christ in the form of sinful flesh is the driving issue for Christology.

Bonhoeffer expressed his notion of Christ's hiddenness through his theology of the humiliated Christ. Bonhoeffer's emphasis on the incarnation in the likeness of sinful flesh means not only that the Christological question shifts, but also that the discussion of the humiliation of Christ shifts. Christ's humiliation doesn't consist in his becoming human, but in becoming human in sinful flesh. The offense of the incarnation is not that God becomes a human; God entering the creation in the form of a human being is just another indication of God's care for and affirmation of the creation. Instead, the humiliation of Christ is that he becomes one like us, truly taking on our fallen flesh.[11]

When Bonhoeffer focuses on the humiliated Christ, he never does so in isolation from the incarnate or exalted Christ. Each of these forms, incarnate, humiliated, and exalted, are proper to the existence of the God-man. However, the God-man in the likeness of sinful flesh 'is necessitated by the world under the curse. The incarnation is related to the first creation; the humiliation is related to the fallen creation. In the humiliation, Christ, of his own free will, enters the world of sin and death. He enters it in such a way as to hide himself in it in weakness and not to be recognized as the God-man'.[12] We see in this an early indication of the scheme we explored in the last chapter, the difference between the created and the natural. For Bonhoeffer, the incarnation is related to the created world; God becoming a human isn't foreign to his being, and therefore God becoming human doesn't simply belong to the sinful world. However, God becoming human in the form of the sinful flesh, the humiliation of the God-man, is necessitated by human sin. Again, to become a human is not humiliating to God; to become a human in the likeness of sinful flesh is. This means that the form of Christ in the natural, penultimate time is the form of humiliation.

This raises for Bonhoeffer the question of the doctrine of Christ's sinlessness, which he describes as 'the central point at which all that is said [about Christ] is decided'.[13] This is of such importance because our understanding of Christ and his relation to the sinful world, and thus our understanding of the central message of Christianity, depends on it. If Christ remained aloof from sin, then Christianity cannot claim that God has redeemed and restored the world. Instead, Bonhoeffer asserts that Christ has truly taken on sinful flesh, and thus, when he went to the cross, he went to the cross as a sinner. But it also means that

> His *sarx* is our *sarx*.[14] It is the very nature of our *sarx* that we are tempted to sin and self-will. Christ has taken upon him all that

> flesh is heir to. . . . He is a man as we are, he is tempted in all points like we are, yet more dangerously than we are. Also in his flesh was the law which is contrary to God's will. He was not the perfect good. At all times he stood in conflict. . . . Beyond recognition, he stepped into man's sinful way of existence.

Bonhoeffer's emphasis on the suffering God is intrinsically tied to his understanding of the hidden Christ. The humiliated Christ suffers with and for the fallen world. In order to overcome human rebellion and reconcile humanity to himself, God, in Christ, has come to earth in the hidden form of the sinful flesh. Christ's suffering is a suffering on behalf of and with human suffering. In the Christology lectures, specifically in Bonhoeffer's theology of Christ's suffering, we see the foundations of the theme of the suffering God who can help.

SUFFERING WITH CHRIST IN *DISCIPLESHIP*

It is in *Discipleship* that Bonhoeffer's understanding of the suffering God, and the disciples' call to suffer with Christ, comes predominantly to the fore. Here, Bonhoeffer speaks deeply and passionately about the cross, and about the participation of the follower of Christ in the cross of Christ. Comments have been made above about the place of *Discipleship* in Bonhoeffer's theological development; despite some of the differences in Bonhoeffer's later work, what cannot be denied is the importance of the suffering of Christ in this work, and that this importance will continue throughout the end of Bonhoeffer's life. In *Discipleship* we see an unadulterated call to take up the cross of Christ, which yields its fruit in its due season in Bonhoeffer's later theological work.

Though Bonhoeffer's focus on the cross can be seen throughout the book, we will focus our attention on chapter 4, 'Discipleship and the Cross'. This is the critical chapter in *Discipleship* for grasping the impact of the cross on Bonhoeffer's conception of following Christ, and for seeing his developing thoughts on the need for the disciple to suffer with Christ through cross bearing. But before we look at this chapter, we must set the stage with a brief look at Bonhoeffer's famous statements in *Discipleship* regarding cheap and costly grace.

To begin the book, Bonhoeffer aimed his guns at the enemy of discipleship: cheap grace. This, he writes, is 'preaching forgiveness without repentance; it is baptism without the discipline of community;

it is the Lord's Supper without confession of sin; it is absolution without personal confession. Cheap grace is grace without discipleship, grace without the cross, grace without the living, incarnate Jesus Christ'.[15] Cheap grace is dangerous because it makes grace into a principle by which people can live lives uninterrupted by the demands of Christ. Cheap grace means 'forgiveness of sins as a general truth', thereby allowing people to live their lives out of this principle without ever confronting their sin, and without them being confronted by Christ.[16] Cheap grace turns discipleship into a bourgeois life, no different from the life of the world that surrounds the disciple.

Bonhoeffer's call in *Discipleship* is the call to costly grace: 'It is costly because it calls to discipleship; it is grace because it calls us to follow *Jesus Christ*. It is costly, because it costs people their lives, it is grace because it thereby makes them live. . . . Above all, grace is costly, because it was costly to God, because it costs God the life of His son . . . and because nothing can be cheap to us that is costly to God.'[17] Salvation is a gift from God, and in one sense it is free: we could do nothing to earn what God has done for us in Jesus Christ. But we must not confuse free with cheap. It is free only in one sense, but it is quite costly in another. It will cost us our lives; however, in losing our lives, we gain life. When Bonhoeffer turns his attention to the disciple and the cross, we see what he means by the above statements. His chapter on 'Discipleship and the Cross' describes the life of the disciple who recognizes the costliness of grace and who would therefore take up the cross.

He begins the chapter by quoting Mark 8:31–38, in which Jesus calls his disciple to deny themselves and take up the cross. Essentially, the rest of the chapter contains Bonhoeffer's thoughts on this call. The important connection that Bonhoeffer makes is that the call to the disciples to bear the cross is a call to participate with Christ in his sufferings. As we have seen in *Sanctorum Communio*, Christ's action as a vicarious representative is an action of entering into human suffering. And, while there were hints of the participation of the church in this suffering, there was no real development of this theme. And, although in the Christology lectures there is a call to participate in the humiliation of Christ, once again there was no true development of the theme. It is not until this stage in Bonhoeffer's theological career that we see such intentional focus on the theme of taking up the cross and following Christ. Undoubtedly this is related to the historical factors of the day: The impact of the Nazi regime and the certain uncertainty of life as a disciple during their reign seems to be unfolding itself in Bonhoeffer's mind. There is a sure inkling that the future is going to call for severe demands from those who would be loyal to Christ, and what it means to participate in Christ's sufferings will not, cannot, remain a theological concept. It will mean concrete action with Christ.

In what is undoubtedly a veiled accusation against the Confessing Church, Bonhoeffer writes that Peter's reaction to Christ with his refusal to believe Christ's statement regarding his impending death reveals that 'from its very beginning the church has taken offense at the suffering Christ. It does not want that kind of Lord, and as Christ's church it does not want to be forced to accept the law of suffering from its Lord'.[18] The problem, of course, is that this *is* the kind of Lord the church must follow. It takes a while for the disciples to comprehend this; Jesus teaches them at numerous places in the gospels that they will suffer with and for him. If he will suffer, so will they. The call to suffer is not only on his life, but is on theirs as well.[19] The suffering that Bonhoeffer speaks of is not a call to a general suffering or random suffering; it is suffering and being rejected with and for Christ. Just as Christ was rejected, so will the follower of Christ. It is in this rejection that the disciple truly takes up Christ's cross, and in bearing the cross the disciple is called to die his death and so be freed to live for the world.

But this happens only through disciples who bear the cross and thus are free for the world, even in its fallenness and darkness. As they follow after Christ by walking in his way, his followers become conformed to his image. But the form is a particular form, the form of the crucified and suffering Christ. We read, 'No one is able to discover the lost image of God unless they participate in the image of the incarnate and crucified Jesus Christ. . . . Only those who allow themselves to be found before God in the likeness of this image live as those with whom God is well pleased.'[20] It is in living this life of the suffering servant that the follower of Christ can be obedient. As such, it is in conformity to the suffering Christ that the disciple is freed for life.

Although Bonhoeffer has not yet made the move to his thinking regarding *etsi deus non daretur*, the theme of the suffering God, and the disciples call to suffer with him, is clear in *Discipleship*. The follower of Christ will be freed to live before God without God only as she is conformed to him through the experience of suffering. In *Ethics*,

Bonhoeffer once again takes up the theme of *Stellvertretung*, a theme that leads straight to the God who is pushed out of the world on the cross.

SUFFERING IN *ETHICS*: VICARIOUS REPRESENTATION AND SUFFERING WITH CHRIST

Earlier, in Chapter 2, we discussed *Stellvertretung*, vicarious representative action, from the perspective of Bonhoeffer's understanding of Jesus Christ as the one who lives the responsible life for others. In turning once again to *Ethics*, we do so to see how Bonhoeffer understands the relationship between suffering and representative action. Bonhoeffer uses *Stellvertretung* as a critical concept in the development of his thinking regarding his activity in the resistance and his ethical thinking more generally. The purpose of this section is not to engage at length in an analysis of Bonhoeffer's ethical reasoning or to offer an evaluation of his actions. Instead, I will engage with the notion of *Stellvertretung* in *Ethics* with the goal of making clear the connection between human participation in the sufferings of Christ and the willingness to suffer with God in bearing the guilt of sin.[21]

We noted earlier that Bonhoeffer's conception of vicarious representative action was developed in *Sanctorum Communio*, at the outset of Bonhoeffer's theological career. It is remarkable how this notion would serve Bonhoeffer's theology through the rest of his career, but just as critically, how it would shape his ethical actions as he opposes the Nazi regime. *Stellvertretung* is in no way merely a theological idea; Bonhoeffer's choice to enter the resistance against Hitler, and to act in ways that are controversial to this day was deeply impacted by the notion of vicarious representative action. He finds himself challenged by the critical questions: How does one follow Christ during the reign of one of the most brutal regimes in human history? What does 'ethics' mean in this context? How does one even begin to grasp how to live ethically in a time when right is called wrong and wrong is called right? The concept of *Stellvertretung* is the means by which Bonhoeffer seeks to answer these questions. Let's turn now to *Ethics* and see how Bonhoeffer connects vicarious representative action and suffering with Christ, and brings these ideas together to form a uniquely ethical vision in the midst of a dark and challenging time.

Bonhoeffer begins *Ethics* by stating that the ethical question is not 'how can I be good?' or 'how can I do good?' but instead 'one must ask the wholly other, completely different question: "what is the will of God?"'[22] This question leads one to approach ethics not from the perspective of laws or principles, but from the perspective of responsible action for others. Responsibility and vicarious representation belong together.[23] In *Act and Being*, Bonhoeffer connects responsibility with transcendence. Transcendence is not the metaphysical absence of God from his creation, but rather is a term of relationships and personhood. The transcendent one is my neighbor, the one whose very being creates upon me a claim of responsibility. My created being is a bordered being, bordered by others. In the face of the other, I am claimed for them and I exist for them. Jesus is the one who has lived his life responsibly for others, and in doing so he has been willing to take on the guilt of the other for the sake of overcoming that guilt. In *Ethics*, we see the ethical activity that this vicarious representation demands of those who would follow the way of Jesus Christ. The one who would follow Christ must be willing to take on guilt, must be willing to bear the cross, and so suffer with Christ in his bearing of guilt for others. Vicarious representative action leads us directly to the suffering of God and therefore to life *etsi deus non daretur*.

In his discussion on 'The Structure of the Responsible Life' in 'History and Good [2]', Bonhoeffer makes the explicit connection between responsibility and vicarious representative action, following along the lines of *Creation and Fall* with its conception of human life as life that is bound to others, both to God and to my neighbor.[24] Bonhoeffer states it plainly: 'Responsibility is based on vicarious representative action.'[25] He then goes on to give examples of what this vicarious representation looks like in ordinary life: the father, the statesman, the teacher of students. So, in the midst of our everyday lives, each person in some way acts as a *Stellvertreter* for others. At the base of this vicarious representative action is the person of Jesus Christ, who demonstrates in becoming our vicarious representative that human life is defined by responsibility for others, or, to say in a different way, to be human is to live for others. As we have seen throughout our study of Bonhoeffer, the problem of human sin is that we have rejected others, we have rejected God and neighbor, and so we refuse to act as representatives for one another and instead we choose to live for ourselves. However, Christ's life gives us the paradigm of the true humanity that recognizes and accepts the responsibility to act on behalf of others. But it is not the conception of vicarious representative in our daily living that is at the heart of Bonhoeffer's view of *Stellvertretung*. It is the cross of Christ that occupies the central place in his understanding of following after Jesus and that creates the call to suffer with and for others that is on all of Jesus' followers.

At the heart of Bonhoeffer's thinking on representation is Christ bearing the cross, the sin of the world, for others. Christ's representation of humanity isn't a general representation but a concrete activity of cross bearing. His representation means that he is willing to take on guilt. Christ enters into the sin of the world, really and truly becomes a sinner, and thus incurs guilt, a theme we saw above in our investigation of the humiliation of Christ in the Christology lectures, which forms the background to Bonhoeffer's reflections on Christ's vicarious representative action in *Ethics*. Christ was willing to enter into the guilt of others and so, too, should those who would follow him. In taking on the guilt of others, Christ has expressed both the 'No' and the 'Yes' of God to reality as he himself is reality. Thus, to follow after Christ by becoming a vicarious representative for others is to act in accordance with reality, which, Bonhoeffer believes, is the main goal of ethics. In his estimation, too many ethical systems have as their end result obedience to principles that end up divorcing their adherents from the real situation before them. These rules and principles can too easily become barriers to responsible action for others. Instead of a willingness to get involved, even if it means 'getting our hands dirty', we hold back, and we justify our lack of involvement through appeals to our rules and principles. But, for Bonhoeffer, since Christ *is* reality we must take all our ethical cues from him, and not put in place *a priori* principles that we can use to keep ourselves clean, it is inevitable that the one who would follow Christ would be called to do as he did and take on guilt in responsible action for others. The incarnation and crucifixion of Jesus shows us the way of responsible life as those who act for others. We read, 'Jesus' concern is not the proclamation and realization of new ethical ideals, and thus not his own goodness . . . but solely love for real human beings. This is why he is able to enter into the community of human beings' guilt, willing to be burdened by their guilt'.[26] Jesus is motivated by love for the real human being, not his ideals or his own goodness. Ethical systems based on rules and principles place ideals and personal goodness as the highest value in ethical matters; not Jesus. He places love for human beings as his highest value and is therefore willing to enter into guilt and suffering on their behalf.

Given that this is the motivation of Christ, shouldn't it also be the motivation of those who follow him? Bonhoeffer puts it starkly: 'Because Jesus took the guilt of all human being upon himself, everyone who acts responsibly becomes guilty.'[27] To live responsible lives for others will mean incurring guilt. To follow the way of Jesus, to bear the cross of Christ, is to enter into the guilt of the fallen world for the sake of bearing that guilt on her behalf. The church becomes a community of those who bear the guilt of the world in responsible action on its behalf. This plays itself out in Bonhoeffer's life through his decision to become a double agent, to lie and mislead. What we see in Bonhoeffer's decision to join the conspiracy and to become implicit in a plot to murder another human being is his attempt to live a life of vicarious representation through cross bearing and taking on guilt. This is critical to understand: He did not choose this course of action because it was the 'right thing to do' but because it was, in his estimation, the responsible thing to do, even though he knew that in doing so he was incurring guilt. Bonhoeffer believes that he is becoming guilty through his actions. But he has seen how the church's desire to keep her hands clean resulted in a church that was unable to vicariously represent those who were suffering under the Nazis. This failure begins with the church's Christology that yields a failed ethic. In his incarnation, Jesus did not remain aloof from the sin and guilt of the world. Jesus' incarnation in the likeness of sinful flesh means that his mission is not to remain clean but to become guilty for the sake of others. The church has failed to recognize this and has therefore failed to act vicariously on behalf of the victims of Hitler, choosing instead to protect herself.

One can see why Bonhoeffer leads *Ethics* by stating that 'how can I be good?' and 'how can I do good?' are the wrong questions to ask. Were those the ethical questions about which he was primarily concerned, he would have undoubtedly made a very different decision regarding his involvement in the conspiracy. However, because of his view that Christ's concern was love for real human beings, his concern was to love those who were threatened by Hitler's tyrannical regime, and so to 'put a spoke in the wheel' through responsible action for others. In speaking of the question of whether it is ethical to lie to protect another, Bonhoeffer writes:

> I come into conflict with my responsibility that is grounded in reality when I refuse to become guilty of violating the principle of truthfulness for the sake of my friend, refusing in this case to lie energetically for the sake of my friend . . . refusing, in other words, to take on and bear guilt out of love for my neighbor. Here, as well, a conscience bound to Christ alone will most clearly exhibit its innocence precisely in responsibly accepting culpability.

To take on guilt is to bear the cross and so enter into the sufferings of the world. As we have progressed through this chapter, we have analyzed Bonhoeffer's conception of the suffering God and the call to those who would be his followers to enter into that suffering. We now return to the theme of this chapter, living life *etsi deus non daretur*, with the context of Bonhoeffer's understanding of the suffering God in his larger theological project.

SUFFERING WITH GOD IN THE WORLD

My goal in this chapter has been to make the connection between Bonhoeffer's notion of *etsi deus non daretur* and the suffering God. In the letter of 16 July 1944, Bonhoeffer connects the rejection of the metaphysical God of power with an understanding of God as the suffering God who can help. In his view, the God of power is a creation of Western Christianity, and at this stage in her history, the Western world has taken leave of the hypothesis of this metaphysical God, the *deus ex machina*. Instead of fighting for the 'God' of power, Bonhoeffer believes that theology and the church now have the opportunity to recognize that in the coming of age of the world and her rejection of the metaphysical God of power there is an opportunity to return to the God of the Bible, the God of weakness and of suffering, and to thus confront the world come of age with *this* God, the true God. Since the world no longer needs the 'God' of power, the church shouldn't try to convince it that it does. Instead, the church should turn once again to the Scriptures in repentance, and there find the God who suffers, and calls for us to enter into his sufferings through cross bearing and vicarious representation for others.

As such, for Bonhoeffer, life *etsi deus non daretur* is the life of suffering with God in and for his world, the world that he has redeemed and forgiven through his sufferings on the cross. In returning to the letter of 16 July, we remember Bonhoeffer's words: '. . . we cannot be honest unless we recognize that we have to live in the world *etsi deus non daretur*. And this is what we do recognize – before God! God himself compels us to recognize it. So our coming of age leads us to a true recognition of our situation before God.'[28] The coming of age of the world has forced the disciple to recognize that her view of God as the power God is false. As the world has come of age and has advanced beyond the need for the metaphysical God, the church is compelled to seek anew the Biblical vision of God. For Bonhoeffer, God himself has superintended this move – 'God himself compels us to recognize it' – and so is calling his church back to the Scriptures to find the God of weakness. The God of weakness is the one who 'would have us know that we must live as men who manage our lives without him. . . . The God who lets us live in the world without the working hypothesis of God is the God before whom we stand continually. Before God and with God we live without God'.[29] Before the weak God and with the weak God we live without the God of power. God still is. God still is God. But he is a different God than we expect. He is not the God of the theology of glory, but is the God of the theology of the cross. He is the God who 'lets himself be pushed out of the world on the cross. He is weak and powerless in the world, and that is the way, the only way, in which he is with us and helps us. Matt. 8.17 makes it quite clear that Christ helps us, not by virtue of his omnipotence, but by virtue of his weakness and suffering'.[30] The letter concludes with a paragraph in which Bonhoeffer draws these key themes together.

> Here is the decisive difference between Christianity and all religions. Man's religiosity makes him look in his distress to the power of God in the world: God is the *deus ex machina*. The Bible directs man to God's powerlessness and suffering; only the suffering God can help. To the extent that we may say that the development towards the world's coming of age outlined above, which has done away with a false conception of God, opens up a way of seeing the God of the Bible, who wins power and space in the world by his weakness.[31]

The world come of age has opened up a new way of seeing God. We live *etsi deus non daretur* as we live without the false conception of God and so live before the weak God.

Bonhoeffer continues his thinking on the weak God in his next letter, dated 18 July 1944. In that letter, Bonhoeffer once again speaks about the suffering God, but turns more to the theme of suffering with Christ as his followers. There he refers Bethge to the poem referred to above, 'Christians and Pagans', and particularly to the line 'Christians stand by God in his hour of grieving'.[32] To stand by God in his hour of grieving is to follow him into his sufferings. We read, 'It is not the religious act that makes the Christian, but participation in the sufferings of God.'[33] We have seen this theme throughout this chapter: participation in the sufferings of God comes about concretely through bearing the cross with Christ. God's suffering is a particular kind of suffering, a suffering that is historical and concrete, a suffering that is particularly located at the cross. When the disciple suffers with God, she does so through cross-bearing: 'That is *metanoia*: not in the first place thinking about one's own needs, problems, sins, and fears, but allowing oneself to be caught up into the way of Jesus Christ, into the messianic event, thus fulfilling Isa. 53.'[34] The follower of Jesus is one who enters into the way of the suffering servant of Isaiah, and in doing so participates with God in his healing of the world.

BONHOEFFER AND LIVING FULLY IN THE WORLD

As we conclude, let us turn our attention once again to the letter of 21 July 1944. We saw this letter in the last chapter, as Bonhoeffer explains with clarity what he means by this-worldliness: 'By this-worldliness I mean living unreservedly in life's duties, problems, successes and failures, experiences and perplexities.'[35] This famous quote continues by connecting this-worldliness with participation in God's suffering in the world. Bonhoeffer goes on to write, 'In doing so we throw ourselves completely into the arms of God, taking seriously, not our own sufferings, but those of God in the world – watching with Christ in Gethsemane. That, I think, is faith; that is *metanoia*. . . . How can success make us arrogant, or failure lead us astray, when we share in God's suffering through a life of this kind?' How indeed? Success and failure seem to lose meaning as the follower of Christ casts herself upon God and into his sufferings in and for the world.

There is a significant irony here regarding the interpretation of the death of God theologians of Bonhoeffer's theology. For Bonhoeffer, Nietzsche was right: God is dead. And yet, it is God himself who compels us to recognize his death. The 'God' of the Christianity that Nietzsche attacked must die. But the death of God for Bonhoeffer is not an ending, it is a new beginning with God. Now the church can recognize that God *was* dead, and died as a weak and suffering God, and though Christ is resurrected, he continues to live on as one who 'wins power and space in the world by his weakness'.[36]

What is the result of this? Life *etsi deus non daretur*. To live life without God before God. The world come of age has given the church the opportunity to rediscover the life that God intends for his children, a life that is marked by freedom and responsibility and vicarious representation as they walk in the way of the cross, and so live the resurrection life of being for others. More particularly, Bonhoeffer envisages a new understanding of Christianity that he labels 'religionless Christianity'. It is to his vision of faith in a world come of age that is described as 'religionless' that we now turn.

CHAPTER 6

RELIGIONLESS CHRISTIANITY

The last chapter outlined the connection between living life *etsi deus non daretur* and the suffering God. In it, we saw that Bonhoeffer's conception of life before God without God takes us to the suffering God, who is weak and powerless in the world, and only as such is the God who helps. This God compels his followers to turn away from the false 'God' of power who is a Western metaphysical construct, and turn toward the God of the Bible, thereby living before *this* God and no other.

The question that we must now ask is: what kind of Christianity arises in the place of the old? If Christianity as we have known it for the great majority of its 2,000-year history has been based on the metaphysical God of power, then what will its form be if it follows after the suffering God? We have seen that we are called to participate in the sufferings of God as we live life as if he were not given. But what kind of faith and life are being suggested through this picture? The answer that Bonhoeffer gives, and which will occupy our attention in this chapter, is one of his most pregnant conceptions: religionless Christianity.

RELIGIONLESS CHRISTIANITY: AN OVERVIEW

We began our thinking together about Bonhoeffer's theology in Chapter 2 by pointing to Jesus Christ as the center of Bonhoeffer's theology, organizing our thoughts around the question Bonhoeffer asked in his letter of 30 April 1944: 'What is really bothering me incessantly is the question what Christianity really is, or indeed who Christ really is, for us today.'[1] Up to this point in our investigation of Bonhoeffer we have focused on the second part of the question Bonhoeffer asks,

'Who is Jesus Christ,' and the implications of this for the church and its relation to the world. Now, we turn to the first part of this question: what is Christianity today? Given Bonhoeffer's questions about Jesus Christ and the way that we must understand him in a world come of age, what happens to Christianity? What does Bonhoeffer envisage the Christian faith will look like in this new world?

In his thinking about religionless Christianity, Bonhoeffer is clearly searching for the core of the Christian faith. What is Western, metaphysical accretion and what is central to the revelation of God in Jesus Christ. This is, in some ways, consistent with the project of his teacher in Berlin, Adolph Von Harnack, whose theology was an attempt to distill the Christian faith to its kernel. However, though the desire is similar, Bonhoeffer's project does not yield a Harnackian answer, nor is Bonhoeffer satisfied with the Bultmannian project to discover the kerygma, the essential message of Christianity, by stripping away the 'mythical' elements that were developed in a pre-scientific, pre-Enlightenment religious setting. What Bonhoeffer wants is a complete rethinking of Christianity as a 'religion' that maintains the 'mythical' but strips away the clothing of Western metaphysics. In fact, Bonhoeffer is effectively asking the following question: Is Christianity a religion? Or, is Christianity as religion an invention of Christendom, which we must now let go of in order to understand it as something completely different? To what degree has conceiving Christianity as a religion led Christianity away from Jesus Christ? Bonhoeffer himself puts it this way:

> Our whole nineteen-hundred-year-old Christian preaching and theology rest on the religious *a priori* of mankind. 'Christianity' has always been a form – perhaps the true form – of 'religion'. But if one day it becomes clear that this *a priori* does not exist at all, but was a historically conditioned and transient form of human self expression, and if therefore man becomes radically religionless . . . what does that mean for 'Christianity'?[2]

If, in the coming of age of the world, humanity no longer needs the religious *a priori* to explain life or to cope with existence, or if humanity come of age no longer needs the *deus ex machina*, then what happens to the Christian faith? What happens to the religion Christianity when humanity moves past the need for religious forms?

More pointedly, Bonhoeffer's concern is seen in the following question found in the letter of 30 April? 'How can Christ become the Lord of the religionless as well? Are there religionless Christians? If religion is only a garment of Christianity – and even this garment has looked very different at times – then what is a religionless Christianity'?'[3] As we progress through this chapter, it will become clear that Bonhoeffer's main concern in asserting a religionless Christianity is to free Christ from the form of religion that has been rejected by the modern world in order to be free to proclaim the Lordship of Christ to the world come of age. But he doesn't do this simply because the modern world is rejecting Christianity, as some kind of defensive maneuver intended to try to connect with whims of the era. We have seen that Bonhoeffer believes that the coming of age of the world is a genuine opportunity for Christianity to open her windows and allow a fresh breeze to clear the air. For Bonhoeffer, the problem with the religious form of Christianity is that it pushed Christ to the edges of life. He was needed when he was needed, when we are facing illness or financial disaster, marital stress or the end of life, but he is not encountered in the center of our lives on a daily basis. The God of the Christian religion is there when we need him in distress, but otherwise is unnecessary for living. The question of how Christ can become Lord of the religionless is the question of how we can once again truly assert Christ in his fullness as the center of 'Christianity'.

Before turning to Bonhoeffer's earlier theology to put his search for religionless Christianity in its context, we must first spend a moment clarifying exactly what Bonhoeffer means by 'religion'. There are two key ideas that mark the 'religious' phase of Christianity: inwardness and metaphysics, both of which share the same problem: both metaphysics and inwardness remove God from his place at the *center of life*. We have well-covered in this book the problems with the metaphysical: God as a metaphysically transcendent other pushes him to the margins, removing him from his centrality in the world. Bonhoeffer counters this notion of metaphysical transcendence through his ethical transcendence, in which transcendence is not to be thought of as a metaphysical abstraction of God 'out there', but instead is the encountering of the other who places a demand of responsibility on me. This is ultimately the encounter of God in the form of Jesus Christ. In encountering the other, we are encountered by God. God became human and so is not to be understood as the one who exists metaphysically 'out there' but to reveal his place in the life of creation.

Inwardness also pushes God out of the center of life and is the opposite mistake of a metaphysics of transcendence. While metaphysics pushes God out to the margins, inwardness brings God into the self in such a way as to remove him from the center of our lives. God 'within' is divorced from our 'natural' lives, to use Bonhoeffer's phrase from *Ethics*. Religion as inwardness makes God necessary only to our 'spiritual' selves, thereby eliminating his place in the daily life of the follower of Christ. God is given a place only over certain parts of our lives, and is paid attention to in religious ways, but the character of the Christian life as a robustly natural and physical life in which God is Lord over all is lost when God is pushed inside. When God is necessary only for 'religious' reasons then his place as Creator and Lord of all of life is lost. Christianity as inward religion has contributed to the loss of God in the modern world. Instead of proclaiming Christ as Lord of all, 'spiritual' and 'physical', the Christian religion has hastened the removal of God from the lives of modern people.

When Bonhoeffer speaks of religionless Christianity, then, it is against this tendency of Christianity as religion that his comments are directed. Bonhoeffer desires a new conception of the Christian faith that occludes the dangers of both metaphysics and inwardness. In other words, Bonhoeffer's notion of religionless Christianity has nothing to do with removing Christ from his centrality in and for the world. On the contrary, through his musings on religionlessness Bonhoeffer desires to once again establish that centrality in a way that traditional Christianity has lost. As such, our purpose in exploring religionless Christianity in this chapter is to see how it emphasizes the centrality of Christ in the world come of age.

In turning now to Bonhoeffer's early theology, we will begin with the Christology lectures, looking at Bonhoeffer's affirmation of Christ as the center of human existence, as the center of history, and as the mediator between God and nature. In this section in the lectures we get a clear statement of Bonhoeffer's understanding of Christ's ontological position as the center of all. Having explored the Christology lectures, we will analyze the mediatorial role of Christ in *Life Together*.

CHRIST THE CENTER: THE PLACE OF CHRIST IN THE CHRISTOLOGY LECTURES

Bonhoeffer's thinking of the place of Christ is connected with his theology concerning the proper question of Christology. Casting our minds back to Chapter 2, we remember that Bonhoeffer challenges traditional Christological constructions on the grounds that they ask the wrong question. Instead of asking the question 'how can Christ be both God and human?' or 'what does it mean that Christ is both God and human?', Bonhoeffer instead would have us ask, 'Who are you?' The question 'who' is the question of the mind that has quit trying to classify Christ as one piece of data among many, and instead recognized his singular place as the Counter-Logos, the one who relativizes human thinking and reveals to us the boundaries of our ability to classify. In other words, the question 'who?' is the only proper question to ask in the face of God's revelation of himself in Jesus Christ.

When he turns to asking the question of the place of Jesus Christ, Bonhoeffer locates the question within the already established primary question of Christology, the 'who?' question. He writes,

> If we look for the place of Christ, we are looking for the structure of the 'Where?' within that of the 'Who?' We are thus remaining within the structure of the person. . . . If this structure can be demonstrated to be existential, and not a chance accidental one, then we shall have theological proof that the mode of existence of the person of the Risen One is in time and space. So we must ask this question 'Where?'[4]

What Bonhoeffer is getting at here is the question of Christ's presence *in* history. The Risen One is not merely one who exists 'out there', beyond time and space, transcending history. No, the Risen One is present in time and space, not as an idea or a piece of data, but as a *person*; this is why establishing Christ's presence in time and space takes on an existential bent. Though Bonhoeffer has engaged with Heidegger in *Act and Being*, he is not here primarily concerned with Heidegerrian existentialism. Instead, he is pushing at the personal presence of the risen Christ in history. We have seen in Chapters 2 and 5 the way in which Bonhoeffer speaks of the *form* of Jesus in history, as the humiliated and resurrected Christ. Here he is asking the question of the *place* where the humiliated and resurrected form is present.

So, 'where does he stand?'[5] Christ stands where I should stand but cannot. Christ stands 'at the boundary of my existence'.[6] But most fundamentally, Christ stands *pro me*. In standing where I should stand, in standing at the boundary of my existence, Christ stands at the center of my existence because he stands for me. He takes my place at the center of my existence and so stands for me. He stands as the mediator between me and myself. As Bonhoeffer has asserted in *Sanctorum Communio* and *Act and Being*, and will assert in *Life Together*, there are no truly unmediated relationships. Christ is the mediator of all and stands between us and all our fellow humans, and between us and God. But Bonhoeffer is here asserting an even more fundamental mediatorial relationship: Jesus stands between me and myself, 'between my old "I" and my new "I"'.[7] He becomes the new center because he himself is the form of the new self, i.e., the form of the new humanity to which the old self is being conformed. The irony here is that to assert Christ as the boundary to my old 'I', the transcendent one who encounters me with God's 'No', is also to assert that Christ is the center, the form of my new 'I' and so the one who proclaims to me God's 'Yes'. Christ is the boundary and *therefore* the center: 'Here Christ stands, in the center, between me and myself, between my old existence and the new. So Christ is at the same time my own boundary and my rediscovered center. . . . The boundary can only be known as a boundary from beyond the boundary. In Christ, man knows it and thus at the same time finds his new center.'[8] One of Bonhoeffer's central claims in his early theology, especially *Act and Being*, is that the human cannot place herself into the truth, into new existence. This placing of the self into the new self only happens through God's gracious act from outside the self. The human in sin receives new life from outside, from Christ through the work of the Holy Spirit. This new life is a gift that is ours through the mediatorial work of Christ. Christ is at the center even of my own existence as the one who grants me new life and separates me from my old self.

Christ's presence in history as mediator takes three forms: Word, sacrament, and community. Christ's form in the world is not a general form, but these particular forms mediate the presence of Christ to the world. As Bonhoeffer writes, 'that is his nature and his mode of existence'.[9]

To this point, Bonhoeffer has established Christ as the mediator of the old and new self and so as the center. But he gets more specific than this in speaking of the particular ways in which Christ's centrality, and therefore his mediatorial role, take form. Bonhoeffer asserts three ways in which the centrality of Christ are seen: He is the center of human existence, the center of history, and the mediator between God and nature. Let's take a look at each of these in turn.

Christ is the center of human existence. We have already seen in our analysis above something of what this means. To bring it to a point: Bonhoeffer suggests that to say that God is the center of human existence is something very different than to say that God is the center of our consciousness or of our personalities. Bonhoeffer's point is not that Christ is the center only if he is recognized to be such; just the opposite is the case. Christ as the center is an 'ontological-theological' statement, not a 'psychological' one. Christ, by his very nature of being the God-man, *is* the mediator, and thus stands at the center of human existence, whether human existence acknowledges that or not. His being at the center of human existence, as we have seen, is part and parcel with the fact that he is also at the boundary of human being. These two concepts, center and boundary, demonstrate that Christ is both judgment and justification, the no and the yes. Christ has fulfilled the law, and so become the 'beginning of [humanity's] new existence, its center'.[10] Christ, then, stands at the center of all human existence as the one who has put to death the old and been raised to life as the new humanity.

Christ as the center of history. Once again, Bonhoeffer is not thinking here in terms of humankind's understanding of Christ's place in history, but in terms of the reality of Christ as the basis of human history, even though this isn't known. History cannot understand itself from within itself. History itself is the working out of a work of God, and if history doesn't understand itself from the revelation of God, then it cannot understand its own purpose. The work of God is a work of promise and fulfillment, and therefore history lives between promise and fulfillment.[11]

But promise and fulfillment take on a very particular aim: the coming of the Messiah. History exists for the sake of this coming, but history cannot of itself fulfill this promise. The hope for a messiah exists everywhere in history, Bonhoeffer says, and throughout history human beings have anointed their own candidates for Messiah. However, there is only one place where the Messiah appointed by God has been seen: Israel.[12] Again, Bonhoeffer states that this fulfillment is not demonstrable from within history, and as such Christ destroys and fulfills expectations at the same time. In the same way that Christ is the center of human existence in both the yes and the no of humanity, so is Christ the center of history in both yes and no. He declares 'no' to all of history's attempts to supply its own messiahs, and in doing so demonstrates that he is the Messiah, who comes from outside history in order to be its center. But this revealing of Messiah is a hidden revealing. This revealing happens in and through the humiliated Christ. As Bonhoeffer says, 'The meaning of history is swallowed up by an event which takes place in the depth and secrecy of a man who is crucified. The meaning of history becomes evident only in the humiliated Christ.'[13] Christ is the overcoming of history, of Adam's history, and so the beginning on a new history, the history of humanity with God as those who are restored to God. Christ is both boundary and center.

Christ as the mediator between God and nature. In this section, Bonhoeffer relates the theme of Christ as the new humanity to the importance of nature, a connection that Bonhoeffer states has been made too little in Protestant theology. Because Christ is the new humanity, he 'shows all other creatures to be old creatures'.[14] As we have seen in *Creation and Fall*, God created the natural world to be free to live under the command of God's Word and under the care of God's steward, the human who itself lived under God's command. However, with the fall of humankind and its rebellion against God's Word, creation has lost its freedom.[15] With the resurrection of Christ, nature itself is renewed, and he is revealed to be the mediator between God and nature.

Christ's mediatorial function between God and nature, and the dawning of her redemption, are clearly seen in the sacraments, an event in which natural elements which exist under the old are taken up and become heralds of the new. In Christ, nature is given a new freedom, and we see a foretaste of this in the sacraments. The sacraments are established by God as proclaimers of the word of freedom, of the newness that is now in Christ. Though in and of themselves they are merely bread and wine, the sacraments are taken up by Christ, the Word, and given freedom to proclaim the newness that has come through Christ, the center of human existence, of history, and the mediator between God and nature.

In our overview of Bonhoeffer's teaching of Christ the center in the Christology lectures, we have seen the importance of understanding Christ's place in Bonhoeffer's theology, and the impact that this will later have when Bonhoeffer turns to religionless Christianity. As has been introduced, at the heart of religionless Christianity is the question of whether Christ can be Lord of the nonreligious as well as the religious, and thus to question the form of religion and its necessity as an expression of Christian faith. Because religion forces Christ to the boundaries, he doesn't occupy the center. As we have seen in the Christology lectures, Christ is on the boundaries, but only insofar as this is connected with his centrality. Religion divorces Christ's centrality from his place on the boundaries, and thus leaves him on his own on the boundaries but no longer the Lord at the center of existence, history, and nature. In the Christology lectures, we can see the outlines of what was to come for Bonhoeffer when he enunciates his vision of a religionless Christianity: Christ, the Lord who is at the center of reality, and who is recognized as Lord in the center of human existence, not merely on the borders of human existence.

LIFE TOGETHER: CHRIST, THE MEDIATOR OF RELATIONSHIPS

We will now take a brief glace at *Life Together* in order to see the way in which Christ the center plays out not only in human existence, history, and nature, but in human fellowship as well, and thus make some points about the ecclesial component of Christ's centrality. This will enable us to better articulate Bonhoeffer's vision of the church and its place in a religionless Christianity when we return to the prison letters at the end of the chapter. The issue that Bonhoeffer addresses in his comments about the centrality of Christ to the Christian community is the issue of mediation. The claim he makes is that in true Christian community, there are no unmediated relationships.

Bonhoeffer places human relationships into one of two categories: the spiritual and the psychic or emotional.[16] By spiritual, Bonhoeffer means a relationship that is created by God's Spirit, who brings the presence of Christ to the individual and to the community, and is built on the Word of God. By the psychic or emotional, Bonhoeffer means the kind of bond between people in communities that comes from 'the natural urges, strengths, and abilities of the human soul'.[17] Emotional in Bonhoeffer's usage doesn't merely have to do with human feeling, but about human urges and desires that aren't created by the Spirit of the resurrected Christ. What differentiates these two kinds of community is the presence of Jesus Christ at the center, or the lack thereof.

The community built on emotional love desires unmediated access to the other. It is essentially self-centered, and seeks after the other for the sake of the self, even if the actions of the self appear to be selfless. What appears to be love and a desire for community is in fact the urges of the human heart as they seek to control the other. Inevitably, for Bonhoeffer, unmediated relationship becomes controlling relationship: '. . . in the self-centered community there exists a profound, emotional desire for community, for immediate contact with other souls. . . . This desire of the human soul seeks the complete intimate fusion of I and You . . . in forcing the other into one's own sphere of power and influence'.[18] The result of this is that the strong gain power over the weak, and what appears to be a desire for true community in fact becomes a place 'where self-centered, strong persons enjoy life to the full, securing for themselves the admiration, the love, or the fear of the weak'.[19]

In the spiritual community, matters are quite different. There, Christ is the center, the mediator of all relationships. Instead of the unmediated relationships which are the desire of the emotional community, in the spiritual community fellowship is mediated through Christ. Because he is at the center of all relationships, those relationships exist from and for him. As such, Christ must direct our fellowship with others and define for us what love means. We cannot know what love is based on a general human love but recognize instead that 'only Christ in his word tells me what love is'.[20] Because of this, in the spiritual community there is true being-for-others because the Word of God is present, and the love for the other comes from God through the community and therefore does not depend on the object of love. The person is loved irrespective of who they are, and so the follower of Christ can truly obey Christ's command to love her enemy because Christ is truly present at the center of the spiritual community as the mediator who stands between all relationships.

As such, in the spiritual community, Christ is truly Lord and his love reigns in the community, not the desires of the individuals.

The community seeks his will for the community, not their own. The individuals together realize that the community, and the other individuals, belong to Christ, and not to themselves, and so the other seeks Christ's good and his will for the whole and for the individuals. In all of this, the Christian community seeks not its own ideal for the community, but God's reality. The ability of a Christian community to 'succeed' depends on 'whether or not it succeeds at the right time in promoting the ability to distinguish between . . . spiritual and emotional community'.[21] In doing so, the community realizes that it lives by faith, not by experience.[22] To live by experience is to need experience in order to sustain community. But to live by faith is to realize that it is Christ alone who sustains community. Bonhoeffer concludes the chapter on community with these words: 'For Jesus Christ alone is our community. "He is our peace". We have access to one another, joy in one another, community with one another through Christ alone.'[23]

In the Christology lectures, we saw Bonhoeffer's ideas concerning Christ being the center of human experience, of history, and the mediator between God and nature. In *Life Together* Christ is portrayed as the center of all true human community, the one who mediates human relationships of love. Now, as we turn to *Ethics*, we will see that this is so exactly because Christ is the reality of all, and as such, to live in reality is to live in Christ.

RELIGIONLESS CHRISTIANITY: PROCLAIMING THE LORDSHIP OF CHRIST AT THE CENTER OF REALITY

We return now to the theme of religionless Christianity having established the connection between Bonhoeffer's development of the centrality of Christ and this crucial theme in his prison letters. The key point that I am making in my presentation of religiousness is the way that Bonhoeffer uses it, not to diminish the Lordship of Christ and his centrality, but to reaffirm his Lordship and centrality. We saw above in the opening section of this chapter the irony that religion has been the means through which Christ's claim to be the center and reality of all, and thus the Lord, has been minimized. Bonhoeffer wonders whether or not religion is a necessary component of Christianity, and asserts that he believes it is not. It was perhaps once necessary, but is no longer. What Christianity must do now is recognize and cast off the form of religion in order to once again speak truly about Christ in a world come of age.

But before we turn back to the Christology lectures, we must investigate more closely Bonhoeffer's claim that an understanding of Christianity as religion moved Christ out of the center. As he continues on in the letter of 30 April, Bonhoeffer has a 'discussion' with Bethge in which he ruminates on the fact that he is more often drawn to religionless people than to religious people, and drawn in the sense of being 'in brotherhood'[24] with them. He states that he is reluctant to speak of God with the religious because the naming of God among such people lacks the ring of truth to it. He goes on to make this comment: 'Religious people speak of God when human knowledge (perhaps simply because they are too lazy to think) has come to an end, or when human resources fail – in fact it is always the *deus ex machina* that they bring on to the scene, either for the apparent solution of insoluble problems, or as strength in human failure, always, that is to say, exploiting human weakness of human boundaries.'[25] In this tendency lies the ironic seed of how 'religion' in fact drives Christ further and further away from life. If God is needed only where there is human weakness and boundaries, then God becomes God only on the boundaries of our lives, and not at the center of our lives. And, as humanity has continued to discover ways of making itself stronger, through curing diseases, improving living conditions, etc., the 'gaps' where God could be posited have become smaller and smaller, and thus our need for God has become less and less. Christianity as religion has demarcated a space for God that is shrinking, and is trying to keep that space open by fighting against the world's coming of age. As we have seen, Bonhoeffer believes this is the wrong tack. For him, the proper approach is to once again claim the Lordship of Christ at the center of life, not on the edges. He writes, 'It always seems to me that we are trying anxiously in this way to reserve some space for God; I should like to speak of God not on the boundaries, but at the center, not in weakness but in strength; and therefore not in death and guilt but in man's life and goodness. . . . God is beyond in the midst of human life. The church stands, not at the boundaries where human power gives out, but in the middle of the village.'[26]

Moving back into the prison letters, now, we can see Bonhoeffer's desire is not simply to affirm the world as it is, but to expose the fact that it is 'godless', thereby confronting the world with God. In his letter of 18 July, Bonhoeffer writes, 'When we speak of God in a "non-religious" way, we must speak of him in such a way that the godlessness of the world is not in some way concealed, but rather revealed, and thus exposed to an unexpected light. The world that has come of age is more godless, and perhaps for that very reason nearer to God, than the world before its coming of age.'[27] Bonhoeffer desires to express the centrality of Christ in a way that exposes the godlessness of the world come of age, but also recognizes, in an echo of Luther, that the godless person is closer to God than the person who is filled with ideas of God but doesn't know God. This is why the world come of age is an opportunity for the church: it is a time for her to reevaluate, to rethink the language of faith in order to once again proclaim to the world come of age the Lordship of Christ in non-religious concepts.

A key to understanding Bonhoeffer's thinking of religionlessness is to recognize that this is as much a hermeneutical question as anything. His desire is to 'interpret in a non-religious sense'.[28] His questions revolve around how to speak the truth of the Gospel and its teaching on 'repentance, faith, justification, rebirth, and sanctification' in a non-religious way.[29] We are reminded here of the words that Bonhoeffer composed for the baptism of his godson in which he speaks of the church being silent for a time in order to pray and act righteously, for the purpose of hearing again from God and regaining her voice. But what he says to his godson is this: 'It is not for us to prophesy the day (though the day will come) when men will once more be called so to utter the word of God that the world will be changed and renewed by it. It will be a new language, perhaps quite non-religious, but liberating and redeeming, as was Jesus' language.'[30] The church must wait upon God for the non-religious words that she will be commanded to speak in due time.

To further our understanding of Bonhoeffer's conception on 'religionless Christianity', it will be helpful to see his critiques of two other theologians whom he commends for their desire to critique religion, but whom he himself critiques for failing in their attempts to do so. I speak here of Barth and Bultmann. Bonhoeffer praises Barth for being the first person to see the problems inherent in religion, but famously criticizes him for his failure to see the job through, resorting to what Bonhoeffer calls 'a positivism of revelation'.[31] A great deal of ink has been spilled on what Bonhoeffer means by this, but it is clear that for Bonhoeffer, Barth's *Church Dogmatics* ends up being a restatement of traditional orthodox theology rather than a thoroughgoing reevaluation of the theology of religion. Bonhoeffer clearly feels that Barth made a good start at the critique of religion with his Romans commentary, but instead of following that line to its logical conclusion, ends up with what, for Bonhoeffer at least, is a restoration of the religious. Bonhoeffer is critical of Barth's 'like it or lump it' dogmatics: 'Barth was the first theologian to begin the criticism of religion . . . but he put in its place a positivist doctrine of revelation which says, in effect, "Like it or lump it": virgin birth, Trinity, or anything else; each is an equally significant and necessary part of the whole, which must simply be swallowed as a whole or not at all.'[32]

The danger of Barth's approach is that he doesn't recognize the varying degrees to which these have import. One must swallow Barth's whole system, or none of it. In critiquing Barth, Bonhoeffer invokes the *disciplina arcani*, arguing that there are degrees of mystery with Christian doctrine, and that these degrees must be understood and 'protected against profanation'.[33] In other words, Bonhoeffer is not here arguing that there are no mysterious doctrines that are worth protecting, but quite the opposite. His criticism is that Barth's 'positivism of revelation makes it too easy for itself, by setting up, as it does . . . a law of faith'.[34] A law of faith, and not Jesus Christ, becomes the center of the Christian doctrine. Barth has replaced religion with the faith of the church and not with Jesus Christ. In doing this, he has left behind the world, forcing it to live from its own resources and not from the proclamation of Jesus Christ. At the heart of Bonhoeffer's concern about Barth's system is that he hasn't taken the world into account, and so his criticism of religion falls flat. For Bonhoeffer, Barth ends up reestablishing religion instead of doing away with it, and the loser in that game is the world.

As for his thoughts on Bultmann, Bonhoeffer is also appreciative of the fact that he recognizes the need to rethink religious concepts, but is critical of his 'de-mythologizing' project. But the reason for his disapproval is somewhat surprising: It's not that Bultmann has gone too far, but that he didn't go far enough. He writes: 'It's not only the "mythological" concepts, such as miracle, ascension, and so on (which are not in principle separable from the concepts of God, faith, etc.), but "religious" concepts generally, which are problematic.'[35] In saying that Bultmann did not go far enough, Bonhoeffer is saying that he missed the mark of what truly needs to be rethought. He goes on to say, 'You can't, as Bultmann supposes, separate God and miracle, but you must be able to interpret and proclaim *both* in a "non-religious" sense. Bultmann's approach is still a fundamentally liberal one (i.e. abridging the gospel), whereas I am trying to think theologically.'[36] Bonhoeffer's belief is that Bultmann missed the mark when he sought to abridge the gospel for the sake of making it speak to the modern person. Bonhoeffer doesn't wish to abridge the gospel, but to be able to proclaim it to those who are non-religious. Bonhoeffer's project doesn't end in a denial of the resurrection, etc., but in a way of proclaiming the God of Jesus Christ in a wholly new and non-religious way. Whereas Barth ends up with a restoration, and Bultmann ends up with an abridged gospel, Bonhoeffer desires to end up with a proclamation of Jesus Christ and his Lordship as the center of all.

We recall the letter of 30 April: 'I should like to speak of God not on the boundaries but at the center, not in weakness but in strength; and therefore not in death and guilt but in man's life and goodness.'[37] As we have walked through this chapter we have seen Bonhoeffer's desire to bring the proclamation of Christ away from the boundaries of life, away from the gaps, and into the center. Christ's centrality is a statement about his very being: he is at the center of human existence, of history, and of all human life, whether his presence there is known or not.

But it is important to note that in bringing Christ to the center, there is still a confrontation with the world come of age because there is a claim of Christ's Lordship over the world come of age. We recall that Bonhoeffer has no desire to gloss over the godlessness of the world come of age, but to expose it to a new light. What is that new light? I believe that the new light is the suffering God of the last chapter. In looking at Bonhoeffer's notion of life *etsi deus non daretur*, we saw Bonhoeffer's thinking on replacing the strong God of metaphysics with the weak God who is revealed in Jesus Christ's suffering and death. The purpose of this is to demonstrate the Biblical teaching that God isn't a strong God to whom we turn in our hour of need, but is a weak God, who we stand by in his hour of need. This is what makes the Christian notion of God fundamentally different from a religious notion of God: a religious notion of God seeks a God of power who helps us in our weakness while the Christian notion of God knows that only the suffering God can help.

But in stating this, Bonhoeffer makes a fundamental reversal: for him, the weak God confronts humanity in its strength, instead of the strong God confronting humanity in its weakness. The weak God, revealed in the humiliation and death of Jesus Christ, exposes the world come of age to a new light. The world come of age must not be forced to think itself to be weak so that it will turn and come to the 'God' of power. Instead, the world come of age should be allowed to be what it is: strong, and in no need of a strong God. But what the world come of age needs in its strength is the God who is weak. This is because the world come of age, in its desire to protect itself from the vicissitudes of nature, has exposed itself to itself. The problem for the world come of age is that she may have created protection from the natural environment, but there is no protection from herself. And this is where the weak Christ confronts the world come of age: He remains God's 'no' to the world come of age even as he is God's 'yes'. He is both judgment and justification, the boundary and the center, the end of the old and the beginning of the new. Bonhoeffer's idea of a religionless Christianity is not a statement that the world has progressed and thus become 'better' but is a call to the church to recognize the mindset of the modern world in order to proclaim to that world the centrality of Christ.

CHAPTER 7

THE PLACE OF BONHOEFFER TODAY

As we turn now to bring our study of Bonhoeffer to a close, we do so with the following question before us: What is the place of Bonhoeffer today? Throughout this book, we have sought to lay out and understand Bonhoeffer's theology by investigating thc various aspects that make up the mosaic. The purpose of this book has been to help the reader be able to see both the big picture of Bonhoeffer's theology as well to help the reader to be better equipped to explore the details of Bonhoeffer's theology with more confidence and understanding. We have sought to accomplish this by laying out three key foundational pieces of Bonhoeffer's thought, Christ, church, and world, and showing the interrelation of these critical theological notions. These then led us in turn to analyze two further motifs in Bonhoeffer: his understanding of life before God without God, and the conception of the suffering God that underlies this motif, as well as his notion of religionless Christianity. We have explored Bonhoeffer's theology from beginning to end in an attempt to diffuse the tendency that exists all too often in readings of Bonhoeffer to take up quotes or passages in isolation and to not understand the theological context from which those quotes arise, or not to grasp the connections between one aspect of Bonhoeffer's thought and the others. If the reader is now better equipped to read Bonhoeffer and be able to make connections across his theology, able to read a passage about Christ and have it raise good questions about the church, or about the world, then this book has accomplished its mission.

Having spent the bulk of this work doing thorough analysis of Bonhoeffer's theology, to close the book we will move into our own time and place and ask: what is the place of Bonhoeffer today? At various times in our investigation of Bonhoeffer's theology we have seen how the historical time and place shaped his thinking and actions. To what degree is Bonhoeffer's theology a product of its time, and to what degree does it transcend his own time and speak to us in ours? Can a theology that was crafted during the Nazi regime, a theology that asked questions in one of the darkest hours of human history, speak to people who exist in another, different, time and place? Bonhoeffer's theology speaks almost entirely about the situation of western Europe in the in early and mid 20th century. To what degree is he a resource for people who live in a global world in which the citizens of the world are more deeply intertwined in ways hardly imaginable to Bonhoeffer? Is his theology a product of Germany in the 1920s–1940s, and therefore best left having spoken powerfully then, but not now?

Given the fact that I have written this book, it can be surmised that I do believe that Bonhoeffer has something important to say to us today, that Bonhoeffer should continue to be an important dialogue partner for theology in the 21st century. And, given the shape of the book that I have written, it can also be surmised that I don't believe we can pick and choose Bonhoeffer's theology as we wish. The fact that Bonhoeffer's words are so easily *quoted* makes it so easy to misunderstand him, or at least to only focus on certain aspects of his thought at the expense of others. Undoubtedly, this tendency exists in reading other theologians as well; but there is something unique about Bonhoeffer that makes him easy prey to people looking for ideas to support their own thoughts.

Perhaps the biggest contributing factor in this is the prison letters. These letters open up a window into Bonhoeffer's thinking about Christianity as it would be shaped after the war, and offer the possibility of guidance for us in our post-Christian, global world. The guidance he offers, however, is not firm and thoroughly worked out; it is partial and incomplete. Thus, to attempt to build a theology from the prison letters alone is to go against the spirit of the letters. Undoubtedly, Bonhoeffer was working to enunciate an important vision about what the proclamation of Christ's Lordship would look like in post-war Germany. The questions that he poses are critical questions that we must think through as we engage a different and constantly changing setting for our proclamation of Christ. However, as has been the thrust of this book, to read the prison letters without the proper ability to see the connections between them and the rest of Bonhoeffer's theology is to run the risk of isolating these statements and making them say something beyond what their author would have intended.

To engage with Dietrich Bonhoeffer's theology means to do the hard work of gaining the full picture. There cannot be short cuts or reliance upon snippets. There can be no 'cheap' readings of Bonhoeffer, only 'costly' readings. To truly have the benefit of Bonhoeffer, we must engage with his theology from beginning to end. The goal of this book has been to help the reader to be able to engage more deeply with Bonhoeffer's theology, and therefore to be able to benefit from him.

What is this benefit? For each one who reads Bonhoeffer, the benefits will vary. What I have said regarding a thorough reading of Bonhoeffer doesn't mean that each person who reads him will come to the same conclusions. There is no doubt that the conclusions I am drawing, and the themes that I have chosen, would not be the ones others would choose. It is inevitable in theology that our own needs and experiences shape our reading of a theologian and provide for us the filter by which to analyze and learn from a theologian's ideas. My goal here has not been to give the definitive interpretation of Bonhoeffer because no such thing exists. But there are critical ways that Bonhoeffer has benefitted me in my journey, and it is to these that I turn in drawing this book to a conclusion.

I want to suggest three themes from Bonhoeffer that we have investigated in this book that are significant contributions to theology in the 21st century. I have chosen these themes not merely for their personal impact on my own journey of discipleship, but also because in many ways these are emphases in Bonhoeffer where he was ahead of his time. His thoughts on the three themes mentioned below have influenced, either directly or indirectly, the trajectory of theology in the late 20th century. Although the term can be overused, one might say that in these areas Bonhoeffer stands as a prophetic voice. The three themes I will highlight are: Christian worldliness, the suffering God, and religionless Christianity. Taken together, each of these will reinforce the overriding theme of the centrality of Christ that we have seen in our study of Bonhoeffer's theology.

Christian worldliness. As we move further into the 21st century, one of the key contributions of Bonhoeffer to Christianity is his emphasis on the importance of the created world. Bonhoeffer has in many ways paved the way for theologians who today are reevaluating the place of the created in Christian theology. Of course, one can think of the burgeoning of ecological theology in the past half-century. In a time of increasing theological attention to environmental concerns, one cannot help but think of Bonhoeffer's work in *Creation and Fall* and see there a prophetic word of wisdom regarding the need for Christianity to think deeply and clearly about the world and about its integrity.

This concern in Bonhoeffer is about not only the world, but also about its inhabitants. Bonhoeffer envisages a Christianity that is at once deeply committed to the person of Jesus Christ and about the world in which he became incarnate. While for many theologians through the centuries 'worldliness' is considered dangerous, as there is a danger of taint from the fallen world. As we have seen, Bonhoeffer in no way diminishes the importance of sin to Christian theology. We cannot look to him if we are looking for a way to water down the theological category of human fallenness. We can find in him no lessening of the impact of sin on the creation, nor can we find in him a desire to define sin simply by highlighting and speaking against certain behaviors. Instead, Bonhoeffer defines sin in terms of the failure of the creature to love God and neighbor, to think first of self. Yes, behaviors arise from this failure, but behaviors are not the essence of sin. Failure to love the other due to a love of self, is the essence. But, for Bonhoeffer, the danger of sin doesn't necessitate a vision of Christianity that is divorced from the world. It is the failure to love God, and therefore to adequately love the world he has created, which is the problem with humans. It is the failure to love the transcendent other who exists outside of me and who is created to be the object of my affection that is the problem. So, there is no solution to this problem in the church divorcing itself from the world and not loving the world with the love of Christ.

But this means a certain kind of worldly engagement. We remember Bonhoeffer's letter of 21 July 1944, the day after the plot to kill Hitler failed. Here are Bonhoeffer's thoughts on the kind of worldliness he envisages:

> During the last year or so I've come to know and understand more and more the profound this-worldliness of Christianity. The Christian is not a *homo religiosus*, but simply a man, as Jesus was a man. . . . I don't mean the shallow and banal this worldliness of the enlightened, the busy, the comfortable, or the lascivious, but

the profound this-worldliness, characterized by discipline and the constant knowledge of death and resurrection. I think Luther lived a this-worldly life in this sense.[1]

In this letter we see clearly the Christological nature of Bonhoeffer's this-worldliness. Jesus gives us the model for what it means to be a human: he loved and lived in the midst of the world, the real world. He didn't stand aloof from sinners, but befriended them. He didn't come to form a new religion or to be a philosopher who reveals new ideas, but came as the Son of God who came to reveal both who God is and who humanity is. In other words, he came to live in relationship with God and to open up others to live in fellowship with God. Jesus was a worldly man. But the worldliness is defined: it is not the worldliness of the shallow, the comfortable, the lascivious; Jesus was worldly in none of these senses. Instead, Jesus was worldly as one who was disciplined and who lived in awareness of death and resurrection. Jesus knew that there would be death, his death, due to human rebellion against God. He knew the suffering that sin and death have brought to human living, but he also knew that there would be resurrection, and that this resurrection was an affirmation of God's love of creation. Jesus was not resurrected as a spirit but as a human being in a body.

Ultimately, what Jesus reveals is that love of God and love of the creation are not incompatible; in fact, they are united. To love God is to love and care for the creation. This is why there is no escapism in Bonhoeffer. Resurrection does not lead the Christian out of the world, but back into the world in a whole new way. Bonhoeffer's focus on resurrection doesn't create a dualism in which this world is left behind or viewed as intrinsically evil. Bonhoeffer's understanding of resurrection creates a community of people who know God and thus live disciplined lives and a constant understanding of death and resurrection.

Bonhoeffer's thoughts on worldliness come to fruition in a passage that we have yet to investigate, but which is appropriate for summing up Bonhoeffer's thoughts on this topic. In his letter of 20 May 1944, Bonhoeffer writes to Bethge regarding the theme of polyphony. In this letter, Bonhoeffer is concerned for Bethge, and identifies what he senses is a tension in his life: Bethge is serving in the Nazi army in Italy, and so is away from his wife and newly born child. Bonhoeffer believes that Bethge is in danger of missing the point of the difficulty of separation. Yes, Bethge should miss his family, but he must also be careful to realize that life, as music, is full of counter melodies, sometimes joyful, sometimes sorrowful. But it is these counter melodies that make up our lives. To find the fullness of earthly life is to recognize that life is filled with these joys and sorrows, and each is brought together into the symphony of our lives. So, while Bethge may not wish to embrace the difficulty of distance from his family, there is melody even in that place of longing and sorrow that is making up his symphony. To fail to grasp that is to be in danger of misunderstanding life, with all its sorrows and joys.

At the heart of the symphony of earthly life is the love of God. Bonhoeffer writes, 'What I mean is that God wants us to love him eternally with all our hearts – not in such a way as to injure or weaken our earthly love, but to provide a kind of *cantus firmus* to which the other melodies provide a counterpoint.'[2] The *cantus firmus* is a musical term that can be translated from Latin as 'fixed song'. In medieval church music, the *cantus firmus* was a piece of existing music around which other melodies were set in order to create a polyphonic setting. The *cantus firmus* created the baseline around which the other musical lines were composed. In adopting this metaphor, Bonhoeffer creates a vision of life in which the compatibility of divine and earthly love are expressed. In a polyphonic musical arrangement, the *cantus firmus* is the organizing baseline; so is it with the polyphonic life. In the polyphonic life, the love of God is the foundation. But this love doesn't forbid love for the world. Love of God and love of the world are not in competition with one another. The polyphony of life is such that humans are created to love God and the world, God and neighbor, and only in so doing are humans truly living the life God creates for them. This life will bring with it many contrapuntal emotions and experiences, many joys and sorrows. But at the heart of the truly human life is a love of God that sets the creature free to love the creation. To love God is to love the world, not in the lascivious way, but in a way that is constantly aware of death and resurrection. This is Bonhoeffer's vision of worldliness.

This vision of worldliness is essential for Christianity in the 21st century. Christianity must live the polyphonic life of worldliness that is rooted in a deep love of God for the creation and the creatures. But this must be a disciplined love that constantly remembers death and resurrection. Bonhoeffer leads us to an understanding of worldliness that sets the disciple of Jesus apart form the world in order to be for the world. Bonhoeffer's worldliness is not a cheap worldliness that allows the disciple to settle into worldly comfort or to allow the world to determine the place of Jesus; this, he says, is the failure of liberal theology. Instead, the disciple is one who recognizes that Jesus is both a gift and a challenge to the world. True discipleship is a demonstration of *true* worldliness. This is the worldliness that the followers of Jesus Christ in the 21st century must offer a world of suffering. And, they do this by following a God who entered into the suffering of the world. This is the second key theme from Bonhoeffer's theology that I wish to highlight.

The suffering God. Our discussion of the God who suffers centered on Bonhoeffer's conception of life *etsi deus non daretur*. This, we asserted, is the way that Bonhoeffer critiques the conception of God as a God of power. The coming of age of the world has opened up for Christianity an opportunity to take leave of the God of power of Western Christianity and once again come to the Biblical God who suffers with and for his people. We saw in Bonhoeffer's understanding of life before God without God, of living as if God were not given, that the God we live without is the God of power of traditional Western metaphysics. The new historical setting affords Christianity the opportunity to realize that God has allowed himself to be driven out on the cross, and that God demands that we live before him as he has revealed himself in Jesus Christ, and without him as conceived as the traditional power God.

Bonhoeffer's vision of the suffering God once again stands before us as a prophetic voice. Following Bonhoeffer's death, in the time when the atrocities of the Holocaust have become more widely known and the question of God in light of the ovens at Auschwitz has intensified, the notion of the suffering of God has become a significant topic in theology. Many theologians have turned to the idea of the God who suffers in order to radically rethink Christian theology. Whereas previously Christian theologians would have affirmed the suffering of Christ on the cross, in the past half-century much theological work has surrounded the ontology of God as a sufferer. In what way did God's entry into suffering mean a true suffering for the entire Godhead? Can we affirm that God the Father suffered, or that only the Son suffered? Is God's entry into suffering an adequate theodicy for those who suffered through the extreme injustices committed in the 20th century?

Bonhoeffer didn't ask some of the theological questions regarding the suffering of the whole Godhead, and of course he didn't live through the war to join the theological reflection on suffering in light of the Holocaust and other atrocities of the 20th century. As such, Bonhoeffer's own theology does not contain adequate resources for all the questions that have faced theologians in the post-Holocaust world. However, what Bonhoeffer does provide for theology is a focus on the suffering God who can help. Though Bonhoeffer did not live to engage the theological conversations after the war, he did see the need for theology to understand that thinking about and with Jesus Christ cannot come from a position of power, but of weakness. Bonhoeffer wrote a theological reflection on Hitler's rule in Germany called 'After Ten Years', in which he famously writes to his co-conspirators: 'We have for once learnt to see the great events of world history from below, from the perspective of the outcasts, the suspects, the maltreated, the powerless, the oppressed, the reviled – in short, from the perspective of those who suffer.'[3] Knowledge of the oppression of the Jews and other undesirables, seeing his students killed in a war few believed in, and becoming a traitor to his country have shown Bonhoeffer a view of history that his privileged position would not normally have afforded. But through these experiences in a world turned upside down, Bonhoeffer does come to see the world 'from below', from the perspective of those who suffer. In other words, Bonhoeffer has seen the world from the perspective of Christ, who came as the suffering God who alone can help humanity in its tragic situation.

Again, we see the centrality of Christ for Bonhoeffer's conception of the suffering God who can help. Traditional Christianity, with its emphasis on the power God, has been embarrassed by the cross. Theologically there was always a place for the cross, but it didn't provide a defining view of God. Luther recaptured the original vision with his *theologia crucis*, but his emphasis was lost in later Protestant theology, and the God of power, the God of glory, was quickly put back in place. Bonhoeffer's vision of life from below has given him the opportunity to see Jesus clearly as the suffering God who alone can help humanity. Humanity come of age no longer needs the God of power to be the answer to unanswerable questions; humanity come of age does not need a strong God who gives aid to human weakness. Instead, humanity come of age needs to be confronted by the weakness of God. It is in the confrontation between the suffering

God and humans come of age that human power is challenged and shown to be what it is, a dangerous illusion. It is in this confrontation that humanity sees power as an intrusion into God's good creation. It is in this confrontation that Jesus Christ calls humanity come of age to let go of the power relationships that result from the relations of the *cor curvum in se* and to instead embrace humanity as intended by God, humanity free for love of the other. This is the humanity who recognizes in the face of the other an ethical transcendence that creates a responsibility for the other. In the pre-fall world, this would be the normal way of things. However, since human sin has entered the world, now those who would follow the way of Jesus Christ do so against the way of the fallen systems of the world, and thus are called to suffer with Christ in his humiliation. To be for the other means giving up the privileges that come with power, and so entering into a powerlessness that yields suffering. In order to proclaim Christ, the church must realize that the view from below is the view of the suffering Christ who alone can confront and transform the *cor curvum in se* to the self for others.

But this suffering isn't merely a suffering of identification with the victims. It is also the willingness to suffer for the prophetic proclamation of Christianity against the powers and authorities who would abuse their power. Christianity cannot be co-opted by any political or sociological ideology. Jesus Christ cannot be adopted by any political party and forced to serve its ideology. One of the primary roles of Christianity is to serve as a witness to the world of the rule of Jesus Christ, and as such the church must be engaged with but not servant to any one political ideology. The Confessing Church had much invested with its power in the governmental system of Germany; for Bonhoeffer, this becomes a detriment to her willingness to truly be a community of prophetic call to the world. At one place, he suggests that the church give up its buildings, and that pastors no longer draw a salary, but work to support themselves as they do the work of the ministry. In the German situation, this is a strongly political statement, as the church is deeply enmeshed with the State. Though he never invokes a strongly developed notion of the separation of church and state along Anabaptist lines, Bonhoeffer's understanding of the church community as a prophetic witness that suffers, if necessary, for its faithfulness to Christ against the political powers sounds more Anabaptist at times than Lutheran. His experience of seeing the world from the underside of history helped him to see the failure of the church that is entrenched in political power to remain faithful to Christ's testimony. The church is called to voluntarily take on suffering in speaking against the powers that be, and in so doing follows the way of the suffering God who can help.

As such, Bonhoeffer's vision of the suffering God is at the same time the vision of a church who would follow God into suffering. This is a church that knows that power and privilege are not the ways of Jesus, and so orders its life accordingly. As Christianity moves into the 21st century, Bonhoeffer's call for the church to embrace the suffering Christ, and in so doing to remain faithful to her witness to Christ. In so doing, the church is able to offer to the world, not solutions to all the world's problems, but the suffering God, who confronts human power with weakness and therefore calls humanity to love the other. Bonhoeffer's writings can be a guide to the church of the 21st century as she desires to maintain her prophetic witness to the world through adherence to the ways of the suffering God who can help.

Religionless Christianity. The final theme I wish to highlight in this final chapter is Bonhoeffer's notion of religionless Christianity. In our chapter on religionless Christianity, we discussed the fact that Bonhoeffer's vision of a religionless Christianity was motivated by his desire to affirm the centrality of Christ in all aspects of life. Bonhoeffer's vision of a religionless Christianity is rooted in his desire to confront humanity at the center of life with Jesus Christ. In his critique of the God of power, we have seen that Bonhoeffer believes this God, the stop-gap God, is no longer a necessary hypothesis for humanity come of age. The questions that once needed God for answer can now be answered by physics, medicine, etc. Because of this, 'God' is pushed more and more to the margins, and so the proclamation of Christ by the church is similarly marginalized.

Bonhoeffer counters this trend, not by trying to convince the world come of age that it has not, in fact, come of age, but by proclaiming the weak God. This, he asserts, is the way to bring Christ to the place where he belongs, to the center of all human life. Bonhoeffer's expression of a religionless Christianity is his means of once again asserting the Lordship of Christ and his centrality to human life and existence. The reason that Christ is viewed as no longer necessary by modern humanity is because Christ has been lost under the coverings of religious garb. Bonhoeffer's desire is to free Christ from the trammels of religion and therefore to once again be able to proclaim his Lordship in the world come of age.

But in order to establish the importance of this conception for the 21st century, we must first ask: was Bonhoeffer right in his analysis of the world? Bonhoeffer believed that the world was moving to a secular time in which God, and all that comes with belief in him, would be left behind. He saw the movement in Germany away from the church and away from Jesus Christ in the late 19th and early 20th centuries and believed that humanity would continue on this trend of rejection of God and of Christianity. But is this how things have turned out? Was Bonhoeffer here also a prophet?

In many ways, Bonhoeffer's understanding of the world come of age has not turned out as he envisioned. Humanity has not, in fact, become wholly 'secular'; in fact, one could argue that we are living in just as 'religious' a time as ever. Bonhoeffer viewed 'the world come of age' from a perhaps too narrow perspective of Western Europe. Yes, Western Europe has continued to grow increasingly less Christian, but in many ways this has not been due to a move to the secular, but to a move to increasing interest in other forms of faith and spirituality. Certainly there is a robust secularity in Western Europe, but the secular society envisioned by Bonhoeffer has not come to pass.

This is even more true when we look at the wider world setting. Certainly, one can question Bonhoeffer's label of the 'world come of age' by realizing that much of the world does not see itself in ways that Bonhoeffer envisaged. Bonhoeffer proclaimed that humanity was becoming less needful of God due to technological advances; this may be true to a limited extent in more technologically advanced societies, but in much of the world, there has been a continued recognition of the humanity's need for God. When one surveys the world today, one would be hard pressed to say that the world has become less religious. This is not the case with the growth of Islam and the growing awareness in the West of the importance of Islam to such a large portion of the world's population. Bonhoeffer's claim is also difficult to substantiate when one sees the tremendous growth of Christianity in Latin America and Africa, with its strong emphases on the charismatic nature of the Christian faith. There is in these places a continuing strong emphasis on the need of humanity for God.

So what does this say about Bonhoeffer's 'religionless Christianity'? Was Bonhoeffer wrong? If so, then to what degree is religionless Christianity a theme that can guide theological conversations in the 21st century? To answer this, we have to again rehearse the goal of Bonhoeffer's religionless Christianity. In this vision, the desire is to strip away the elements of Christianity that were not, in fact, central to the original vision of Christ that his disciples lived out early in the history of the church, but which has accumulated over the years under the guise of 'religion'. In my view, what is important about Bonhoeffer's view of religionless Christianity is not whether or not he was an accurate predictor of the future of the world following his death, but whether or not his was an accurate view of the history of Christianity and the way that Christ's original vision of the community, and the communities' original vision of Christ, has been buried under the sediment of religious forms. In this, Bonhoeffer was accurate, and his view of religionless Christianity as that which would set aside old forms that aren't central to her proclamation of Christ's Lordship and that in fact has led Christianity to present that Lordship in ways that are foreign to the Scriptures. The triumphalist Christianity of the West that has touted the God of power has led the church to confuse Christ and Caesar, and has given the church a distorted view of her own way of ruling. The church has adopted a power God and has therefore become a power church. Bonhoeffer believes this is an error rooted in 'religion', and would rather turn the church back to the suffering God who sets humans free, not to be religious, but to live. At the heart of Bonhoeffer's vision of religionless Christianity is the love of life and creation that we looked at in our first theme above. The weak God sets humans free from the bonds of religion in order to be free for life. This life consists in a love for God and neighbor which is the ethical life. To be free for others is to be free for life in God's creation. An embrace of the suffering God is an embrace of life; religion is a failure to truly live the free life that God grants through creation and redemption.

CONCLUSION

In these concluding remarks, I have suggested three themes from Bonhoeffer that theology can learn from as it moves into the early 21st century. These themes arise from the overall mosaic of Bonhoeffer's theology that I have described in this book. Starting with the centrality of Christ and the revelation of humanity found in his incarnation, death, and resurrection, we have discovered in Bonhoeffer an emphasis on the church as the place where the life of Christ is being created in history by the work of the Holy Spirit. The life of Christ is a life for others, in which the other is recognized and valued as my boundary, and so one who transcends me and places a responsibility on me to love and live for others. This life sets the one who would follow Christ free to love God's creatures, which he created and which he has proclaimed worthy of love through the incarnation of Jesus Christ. To be a follower of Christ, to be the community of the church, is to value the creation and to love God's world.

Bonhoeffer believes that the true understanding of God which can guide Christianity forward is to recognize and take seriously the suffering of Christ as a revelation of the God who can help. The world does not need power, but people who are willing to follow Christ and suffer with him. In doing so, those who walk in the way of Jesus fight the tendencies to allow the Christian faith to devolve into religion, claiming instead a different form for Christianity, a form that is, in fact, the form of Jesus Christ, the incarnate, crucified, and resurrected Lord. Bonhoeffer's call to the German church after the war was to be a community of those who truly were taking on the form of Jesus Christ; that call continues to go forward today. Bonhoeffer's challenge that calls humanity to follow after Christ in living for others, in living in the world with its joy and sorrows, is a call that the church, and the world, still need to hear. My hope is that this book will enable readers to better grasp, and so be better equipped, to respond to the challenge that Bonhoeffer's lays before us.

NOTES

CHAPTER 1. BONHOEFFER: INTRODUCING HIS LIFE AND THINKING

1 Sabine Leibholz Bonhoeffer has written a memoir of the family entitled *Verlangen erlebt überwunden: Schicksale der Familie Bonhoeffer* (Gütersloh: Gütersloher Verlagshaus, 1976). Perhaps it is appropriate, given Bonhoeffer's later emphasis on community, that he was born *in communio.*
2 Eberhard Bethge, *Dietrich Bonhoeffer: A Biography*, ed. Victoria Barnett (Minneapolis: Fortress Press, 2000), 15–17.
3 Bethge, *Bonhoeffer*, 3–13.
4 For instance, she is known to have been reading Karl Barth in the mid-1920s as Bonhoeffer himself was becoming familiar with this new theologian on the horizon.
5 Bethge, *Bonhoeffer*, 36.
6 Ibid., 37.
7 See Clifford Green, *Bonhoeffer: A Theology of Sociality* (Grand Rapids, Mich.: Eerdmans Press, 1999), 140ff.
8 Bonhoeffer, *Sanctorum Communio*, ed. Clifford J. Green, trans. Reinhard Krauss and Nancy Lukens, vol. 1 in *Dietrich Bonhoeffer Works* (Minneapolis: Fortress Press, 1998).
9 Bonhoeffer, 'Protestantism without Reformation' in *No Rusty Swords*, ed. Edwin H. Robertson, trans. Edwin H. Robertson and John Bowden (London: Collins, 1965).
10 Bonhoeffer, *Creation and Fall: A Theological Exposition of Genesis 1–3,* ed. John W. de Gruchy, trans. Douglas Stephen Bax, vol. 3 in *Dietrich Bonhoeffer Works* (Minneapolis: Fortress Press, 1997).
11 Keith Clements, *Bonhoeffer in Britain* (London: Churches Together in Britain and Ireland, 2006). This book is a rarity: a theology book with pictures!
12 Bethge, *Bonhoeffer*, 419.
13 Bonhoeffer, *Conspiracy and Imprisonment: 1940–1945*, ed. Mark S. Brocker, trans. Lisa Dahill, vol. 16 in *Dietrich Bonhoeffer Works* (Minneapolis: Fortress Press, 2006), 265.
14 Bonhoeffer, *Ethics*, ed. Clifford Green, trans. Reinhard Krauss, Charles C. West, and Douglas W. Stott, vol. 6 in *Dietrich Bonhoeffer Works* (Minneapolis: Fortress Press, 2005).
15 Bonhoeffer, *Ethics*, 47.

16 See Stephen Haynes, *The Bonhoeffer Phenomenon* (London: SCM Press, 2004) for an overview of various theological approaches to finishing Bonhoeffer's project.
17 Most obvious are the radical theologians of the 1960s, who almost entirely disregarded Bonhoeffer's earlier theology in adopting his 'theology of the death of God'.

CHAPTER 2. 'WHO IS JESUS CHRIST FOR US TODAY?': THE CENTRALITY OF CHRIST IN BONHOEFFER'S THEOLOGY

1 Bonhoeffer, *Letters and Papers from Prison*, ed. Eberhard Bethge (London: SCM Press, 1971), 279.
2 Ibid., 280.
3 Ibid., 279.
4 Ibid., 280.
5 Bonhoeffer, *Sanctorum Communio*, 33.
6 Ibid., 32.
7 Ibid., 33.
8 Green, *Bonhoeffer*, 1.
9 Bonhoeffer, *Sanctorum Communio*, 34.
10 In particular, Bonhoeffer addresses the divergences between a Christian notion of person and four philosophical models of defining social basic-relations: Aristotelianism, Stoicism, Epicureanism, and idealism, including Descartes, Kant, and Hegel, among others. *Sanctorum Communio*, 36–43.
11 Ibid., 49.
12 Ibid., 51.
13 Ibid., 55.
14 Bonhoeffer, *Act and Being*, ed. Wayne Whitson Floyd, trans. H. Martin Rumscheidt (Minneapolis: Fortress Press, 1996), 136ff.
15 Bonhoeffer, *Act and Being*, 91.
16 Ibid., 111–112.
17 See also Bonhoeffer's lecture 'The Leader and the Individual in the Younger Generation', in *No Rusty Swords*, 190–204.
18 Bonhoeffer's theology of sin is addressed in *Sanctorum Communio*, but receives a more thorough analysis in *Creation and Fall*, a book that was based on Bonhoeffer's lectures on Genesis in the winter semester of 1932–1933, a few months before the Christology lectures. These lectures, then, form a backdrop to the Christology lectures.
19 Bonhoeffer, *Christ the Center* (New York: Harper and Row, 1978), 28.
20 Ibid., 29.
21 Ibid.
22 Ibid., 30.
23 Ibid.
24 Bonhoeffer criticizes Schleiermacher and Ritschl for not allowing the resurrection to shape their Christologies. Ibid., 43.

25 Ibid.
26 Romans 8:3.
27 This is an interesting parallel in method to the Christology lectures, where Bonhoeffer begins with the present Christ, and only then does he speak of the historical Christ. In the Christology lectures, it is only by knowing the resurrected Christ who testifies to his historicity.
28 Bonhoeffer, *Creation and Fall*, 145–146.
29 Bonhoeffer, *Discipleship*, ed. Geffrey B. Kelly and John D. Godsey, trans. Barbara Green and Reinhard Krauss (Minneapolis: Fortress Press, 2001), 57.
30 Ibid., 45. Italics in text.
31 Ibid., 57.
32 Ibid., 59.
33 Mark 8:34.
34 Ibid., 85.
35 Ibid.
36 Ibid.
37 Ibid., 205.
38 Bonhoeffer, *Ethics*, 257.
39 Ibid.
40 Ibid., 258.

CHAPTER 3. 'THE CHURCH IS THE CHURCH ONLY WHEN IT EXISTS FOR OTHERS': BONHOEFFER'S ECCLESIOLOGY

1 Bonhoeffer, *Letters and Papers*, 382.
2 Bonhoeffer, 'Thoughts on the Day of the Baptism of Dietrich Wilhelm Rütiger Bethge' in *Letter and Papers*, 300.
3 For a fuller treatment of the idea of transformation in Bonhoeffer's theology, see my 'Death Together: Thanatology and Sanctification in the Theology of Dietrich Bonhoeffer', Unpublished PhD Thesis, Cambridge University, 2007. The material from this section follows chapter 4 in that work.
4 Bonhoeffer consistently uses the Lutheran notion of the *cor curvum in se*, 'the heart turned in on itself'. Humanity, which was created to live as God's creature in loving community, has instead become imprisoned in self-love, and thus unable to live the ecstatic life that was ours by divine gift.
5 Bonhoeffer, *Sanctorum Communio*, 141. Italics in original.
6 Ibid., 157.
7 Ibid., 158.
8 Bonhoeffer, *Life Together and Prayerbook of the Bible*, ed. Geffrey B. Kelly, trans. Daniel W. Bloesch and James H. Burtness, vol. 5 in *Dietrich Bonhoeffer Works* (Minneapolis: Fortress Press, 1996), 28.
9 Ibid.
10 There is a prophetic irony in Bonhoeffer's statements here regarding not taking for granted that one can gather with a body of fellow believers;

he himself would spend the last two years of his life unable to participate in life together with fellow Christians gathered around the Word and sacrament.

11 Ibid., 33.
12 Bonhoeffer uses the terms 'emotional' and 'psychic' interchangeably.
13 Bonhoeffer, *Life Together*, 41.
14 Ibid., 42.
15 Ibid., 43.
16 Bonhoeffer, *Discipleship*, 207.
17 Ibid., 216.
18 Ibid., 220.
19 Bonhoeffer, *Ethics*, 193.
20 Bonhoeffer, *Discipleship*, 225.
21 Ibid., 253.
22 Bonhoeffer, *Letter and Papers*, 336.
23 Ibid., 337.
24 John Matthews rightly argues that this is the correct translation of this term, rather than secret discipline. See Matthews, *Anxious Souls Will Ask* (Grand Rapids, Mich.: Eerdmans Press, 2005), 59.
25 Pangritz, 'Aspekte der "Arkandisziplin" bei Dietrich Bonhoeffer' in *Theologische Literaturzeitung* 9 (September 1994): 756–768.
26 Matthews, 'Responsible Sharing of the Mystery of Christian Faith: *Disciplina Arcani* in the Life and Theology of Dietrich Bonhoeffer', in *Reflections on Bonhoeffer: Essays in Honor of F. Burton Nelson*, ed. Geffrey C. Kelly and C. John Weborg (Chicago, Ill.: Covenant Publications, 1999), 114.
27 Ibid.
28 Ibid.
29 Matthews, *Anxious Souls*, 59.

CHAPTER 4. THE WORLD COME OF AGE: WORLDLINESS IN BONHOEFFER

1 Bonhoeffer, *Letters and Papers*, 326.
2 Ibid., 325.
3 Ibid., 326.
4 Ibid., 327.
5 Ibid.
6 Bonhoeffer, *Barcelona, Berlin, New York: 1928–1931*, ed. Clifford Green, trans. Douglas W. Stott (Minneapolis: Fortress Press, 2008), 359–378.
7 Ibid., 359–360.
8 Ibid.
9 Ibid., 363.
10 Ibid., 365.
11 Ibid., 378.
12 Charles Marsh, *Reclaiming Dietrich Bonhoeffer* (Oxford: Oxford University Press, 1994), 32.

13 Ibid.
14 Ibid., 13.
15 *Act and Being*, 104.
16 For more on Bonhoeffer's notion of freedom, see Ann L. Nickson, *Bonhoeffer on Freedom: Courageously Grasping Reality* (Oxford: Ashgate Press, 2002).
17 Marsh, *Reclaiming Dietrich Bonhoeffer*, 15.
18 Ibid.
19 Ibid.
20 Bonhoeffer, *Act and Being,* 110.
21 Ibid., 112.
22 Ibid., 113.
23 Ibid.
24 Ibid.
25 Bonhoeffer, *Creation and Fall*, 36.
26 Ibid., 40.
27 Ibid., 39.
28 Ibid., 41.
29 Ibid., 64.
30 Bonhoeffer, *Ethics,* 50.
31 Ibid., 51–54.
32 Ibid., 54.
33 Bonhoeffer, *Ethics*, 229. Emphasis Bonhoeffer's.
34 Ibid., 171–172.
35 Ibid., 172.
36 Ibid., 173.
37 Ibid.
38 Ibid.
39 Ibid., 147.
40 Ibid.
41 Ibid., 151.
42 Ibid., 388.
43 Ibid., 389.

CHAPTER 5. *ETSI DEUS NON DARETUR*: LIVING WITHOUT GOD BEFORE GOD

1 Bonhoeffer, *Letters and Papers*, 360.
2 Ibid.
3 Ibid.
4 Ibid., 361. 'God from the machine'. This was a theatrical term in Greek theater, and was a device used to bail the hero out of certain doom. A god would appear and would lift the character out of the immediate peril. Bonhoeffer is concerned that Western Christianity has created such god, who exists for us in our troubles and weaknesses, a god who is a 'stop-gap' God used to explain the unexplainable.
5 Ibid., 348–349. Translation mine.

6 Ibid., 361.
7 Ibid.
8 Ibid., 360.
9 Bonhoeffer, *Christ the Center*, 45–46.
10 Ibid.
11 Ibid., 46.
12 Ibid., 107.
13 Ibid.
14 *Sarx* is the Greek for flesh.
15 Bonhoeffer, *Discipleship*, 44.
16 Ibid., 43.
17 Ibid., 45.
18 Ibid., 85.
19 Ibid.
20 Ibid., 284.
21 See Christine Schliesser, *Everyone Who Acts Responsibly Becomes Guilty. The Concept of Accepting Guilt in Bonhoeffer: Reconstruction and Critical Assessment* (Neukirschener Verlag, 2006).
22 DBWE 6:47.
23 Schliesser, 122.
24 DBWE 6:257.
25 Ibid.
26 Bonhoeffer, *Ethics*, 275.
27 Ibid.
28 Bonhoeffer, *Letter and Papers*, 360.
29 Ibid.
30 Ibid., 360–361.
31 Ibid., 361.
32 Ibid.
33 Ibid.
34 Ibid., 361–362.
35 Ibid., 370.
36 Ibid., 361.

CHAPTER 6. RELIGIONLESS CHRISTIANITY

1 Bonhoeffer, *Letter and Papers*, 279.
2 Ibid., 280.
3 Ibid.
4 Bonhoeffer, *Christ the Center*, 59–60.
5 Ibid., 61.
6 Ibid.
7 Ibid.
8 Ibid., 62.
9 Ibid.
10 Ibid., 63.
11 Ibid.

12 Recall that this lecture is given in the summer of 1933, as Hitler is consolidating his power. To speak of Israel as the place where God has revealed his Messiah was not a politically expedient thing to do, to say the least.
13 Bonhoeffer, *Christ the Center*, 64.
14 Ibid.
15 Ibid.
16 Bonhoeffer, *Life Together*, 38.
17 Ibid., 38.
18 Ibid., 41.
19 Ibid.
20 Ibid., 43.
21 Ibid., 45.
22 Ibid., 47.
23 Ibid.
24 Ibid., 281.
25 Ibid., 281–282.
26 Ibid., 282.
27 Bonhoeffer, *Letters and Papers*, 362.
28 Ibid., 285.
29 Ibid.
30 Ibid., 300.
31 Ibid., 280, 286.
32 Ibid., 286.
33 Ibid.
34 Ibid.
35 Ibid., 285.
36 Ibid.
37 Ibid., 282.

CHAPTER 7. THE PLACE OF BONHOEFFER TODAY

1 Bonhoeffer, *Letter and Papers*, 369.
2 Ibid., 303.
3 Bonhoeffer, 'After Ten Years' in *Letters and Papers*, 17.

BIBLIOGRAPHY

Bethge, Eberhard. *Dietrich Bonhoeffer: A Biography*. Edited by Victoria Barnett. Minneapolis: Fortress Press, 2000.

Bonhoeffer, Dietrich. *Act and Being*. Edited by Wayne Whitson Floyd. Translated by H. Martin Rumscheidt. Minneapolis: Fortress Press, 1996.

— *Barcelona, Berlin, New York: 1928–1931*. Edited by Clifford Green. Translated by Douglas W. Stott. Minneapolis: Fortress Press, 2008.

— *Christ the Center*. New York: Harper and Row, 1978.

— *Conspiracy and Imprisonment: 1940–1945*. Edited by Mark S. Brocker. Translated by Lisa Dahill. Volume 16 in *Dietrich Bonhoeffer Works*. Minneapolis: Fortress Press, 2006.

— *Creation and Fall: A Theological Exposition of Genesis 1–3*. Edited by John W. de Gruchy. Translated by Douglas Stephen Bax. Volume 3 in *Dietrich Bonhoeffer Works*. Minneapolis: Fortress Press, 1997.

— *Discipleship*. Edited by Geffrey B. Kelly and John D. Godsey. Translated by Barbara Green and Reinhard Krauss. Minneapolis: Fortress Press, 2001.

— *Ethics*. Edited by Clifford Green. Translated by Reinhard Krauss, Charles C. West, and Douglas W. Stott. Volume 6 in *Dietrich Bonhoeffer Works*. Minneapolis: Fortress Press, 2005.

— 'The Leader and the Individual in the Younger Generation'. In *No Rusty Swords*. Edited by Edwin H. Robertson. Translated by Edwin H. Robertson and John Bowden. London: Collins, 1965, pp. 190–204.

— *Letters and Papers from Prison*. Edited by Eberhard Bethge. London: SCM Press, 1971.

— *Life Together and Prayerbook of the Bible*. Edited by Geffrey B. Kelly. Translated by Daniel W. Bloesch and James H. Burtness. Volume 5 in *Dietrich Bonhoeffer Works*. Minneapolis: Fortress Press, 1996.

— 'Protestantism without Reformation'. In *No Rusty Swords*. Edited by Edwin H. Robertson. Translated by Edwin H. Robertson and John Bowden. London: Collins, 1965, pp. 92–118.

— *Sanctorum Communio*. Edited by Clifford J. Green. Translated by Reinhard Krauss and Nancy Lukens. Volume 1 in *Dietrich Bonhoeffer Works*. Minneapolis: Fortress Press, 1998.

Bonhoeffer, Sabine Leibholz. *Verlangen erlebt überwunden: Schicksale der Familie Bonhoeffer*. Gütersloh: Gütersloher Verlagshaus, 1976.

Clements, Keith. *Bonhoeffer in Britain*. London: Churches Together in Britain and Ireland, 2006.

Green, Clifford. *Bonhoeffer: A Theology of Sociality*. Grand Rapids, Mich.: Eerdmans Press, 1999.

Haynes, Stephen. *The Bonhoeffer Phenomenon*. London: SCM Press, 2004.

Lawrence, Joel. 'Death Together: Thanatology and Sanctification in the Theology of Dietrich Bonhoeffer'. Unpublished PhD Dissertation. Cambridge University, 2007.

Marsh, Charles. *Reclaiming Dietrich Bonhoeffer*. Oxford: Oxford University Press, 1994.

Matthews, John. *Anxious Souls Will Ask*. Grand Rapids, Mich.: Eerdmans Press, 2005.

— 'Responsible Sharing of the Mystery of Christian Faith: *Disciplina Arcani* in the Life and Theology of Dietrich Bonhoeffer'. In *Reflections on Bonhoeffer: Essays in Honor of F. Burton Nelson*. Edited by Geffrey C. Kelly and C. John Weborg. Chicago, Ill.: Covenant Publications, 1999, pp. 114–126.

Nickson, Ann L. *Bonhoeffer on Freedom: Courageously Grasping Reality*. Oxford: Ashgate Press, 2002.

Pangritz, Andreas. '*Aspekte der "Arkandisziplin" bei Dietrich Bonhoeffer*'. In *Theologische Literaturzeitung* 9. September 1994.

Schliesser, Christine. *Everyone Who Acts Responsibly Becomes Guilty. The Concept of Accepting Guilt in Bonhoeffer: Reconstruction and Critical Assessment*. Neukirschener Verlag, 2006.

INDEX